P9-DGC-538

OTHER BOOKS BY NAURA
HAYDEN

The Hip, High-Prote, Low-Cal,
Easy-Does-It Cookbook

Everything You've Always Wanted to Know
About Energy But Were Too Weak to Ask

ISLE OF VIEW

VIEW

by

Naura Hayden

ARBOR HOUSE
NEW YORK

Copyright © 1980 by Naura Hayden

All rights reserved, including the right of reproduction in whole or in part in any form. Published in the United States of America by Arbor House Publishing Company and in Canada by Clarke, Irwin & Company, Ltd.

Library of Congress Catalog Card Number: 79-56016

ISBN: 0-87795-257-4

Manufactured in the United States of America

The author gratefully acknowledges permission to reprint from the following:
The Future of Marriage by Jessie Barnard. World Publishing Company. Copyright © 1972 by Jessie Barnard. Reprinted by permission of the publisher.
Advice From A Failure by Jo Coudert. Stein and Day. Copyright © 1965 by Jo Coudert. Reprinted by permission of the publisher.
Excerpts from *The Prophet* reprinted from *The Prophet* by Kahlil Gibran, with permission of the publisher, Alfred A. Knopf, Inc. Copyright 1923 by Kahlil Gibran and renewed 1951 by Administrators C.T.A. of Kahlil Gibran estate and Mary G. Gibran.
"Warning: Falling In Love May Be Hazardous To Your Health" by Elizabeth Kaye. Copyright © 1978 reprinted by permission of Russell & Volkening as agent for Elizabeth Kaye. Copyright © 1978 reprinted by permission of *Family Health Magazine*.
"Syntonic Therapy: A Total Approach to the Treatment of Mental and Emotional Disturbances" by Dr. Robert Kronemeyer, *Psychotherapy: Theory, Research and Practice* magazine. Reprinted by permission of the author.

Excerpt from *No-Fault Marriage: The New Technique of Self Counseling and What It Can Do to Help You* by Marcia Lasswell and Norman M. Lobsenz. Doubleday and Company. Copyright © 1976 by Marcia Lasswell and Norman M. Lobsenz. Reprinted by permission of Doubleday and Company, Inc.
On Caring by Milton Mayeroff. Harper & Row. Copyright © 1971 by Milton Mayeroff. Reprinted by permission of Harper & Row Publishers, Inc.
Emotional Common Sense by Rolland S. Parker. Harper & Row.
Copyright © 1973 by Rolland S. Parker. Reprinted by permission of Harper & Row Publishers, Inc.
"The New Sexual Myths" by Dr. Wardell B. Pomeroy. Copyright © 1977 by *McCall's*. Reprinted with permission of *McCall's*.
The Doctor's Book of Vitamin Therapy by Dr. Harold Rosenberg and A. N. Feldzamen, Ph.D. G. P. Putnam's Sons. Copyright © 1974 by Dr. Harold Rosenberg and A. N. Feldzamen, Ph.D. Reprinted by permission of the publisher.
"You Need Body Contact With Others: It Satisfies Skin Hunger" by Barbara Lang Stern. Courtesy *Vogue*. Copyright © 1979 Condé Nast Publications, Inc.
"I'm For The Achiever" by Miller Upton. Reprinted by permission of Sunshine Press.
Self Creation by George Weinberg. St. Martin's Press, Inc. Copyright © 1978 by GHW Theory Corporation. Reprinted by permission of St. Martin's Press.
Small Town by Sloan Wilson. Arbor House Publishing Company. Copyright © 1978 by Sloan Wilson. Reprinted by permission of Arbor House Publishing Company.
You by Frances Wilshire. De Vorss & Company, Inc. Copyright © 1935 by Frances Wilshire. Reprinted by permission of De Vorss & Company, Inc.

WARNING: This book full of Love Energy will change your life!

Contents

Foreword

I'VE BEEN LOVED and I've been unloved . . . Loved is better.

Sophie Tucker said that about being rich and poor and how rich is better, but I consider love infinitely more important than money.

Is there one person on the face of earth who doesn't need love? Can we find just one person who can exist without the love of something or someone? Do you know a taxi driver or a taxidermist who can? Is there an electrician or a plumber, a minister (prime or Methodist), a schoolteacher, a Wall Street banker, a rock singer (or collector), a gardener, a real estate broker, a football halfback, a major (drum or army), a bus driver, an operator (telephone or bigtime), a mailman, a schoolkid—is there anyone who doesn't need love?

No.

Now lots of times we *think* we can exist without love—like when we break up with a spouse or lover and we're all upset and angry, and we build a wall around our feelings for a while; but then, when we realize that only makes us *more* unhappy, we start to allow a few bricks to crumble until finally the whole wall comes down and we're happy once again.

I literally can't exist without love and I thought I was some sort of an exception. Oh, sure, I know lots of people say they can't live without love, but I thought maybe they were just saying that to appear romantic or something. Then, when I started touring with my "Energy" book all over the United States and Canada and Australia, thousands of people would call up the talk shows on radio and TV and tell me heartbreaking stories about how they were trying to cope with a breakup, or how they were trying to hold a marriage or a relationship together because they were petrified of losing the little bit of love they were hanging onto, and suddenly I realized that although *everyone* needs some kind of love, there are millions who find it difficult to get along when love shatters.

No one wants to be a victim, but lots of us find ourselves victimized. You'd be astounded at some of the stories I heard on my tour—sad stories, ridiculous stories, outrageous stories—all related to love. These were ordinary people, like you and me.

Now I've been trying to figure out how to handle love problems for a while, and I've come up with some pretty workable solutions. They've worked for me, and I know that if you apply just a little bit of what you'll read in the next few chapters, you can change the direction of your love life—and your whole life—once and for all. That's why I've written this book—because I feel I've learned a lot and brought myself a long way (about a million miles from where I started), and I feel I can help bring a little happiness to all the potential lovers in the world. Just try some of my ideas. If they helped me, they might help you, and I know that if you really want to change your love life—and your whole life —and you really do apply what you read, you will. Then you can look forward to giving and receiving all the love and joy and good things in life that you deserve.

To Love . . .
Which is God . . .
Which is Love . . .
Which is God . . .

Introduction

ARE YOU A victim of love?

Is your sex life rotten and unsatisfying?

Or did you just think to yourself, "What sex life?"

Are you the dumper or the dumpee of a bad marriage?

Did your last love affair go up in smoke just when you thought you'd finally found someone who made up the other half of your team?

Are you angry a lot at your spouse or roomie; do you find yourself yelling or being yelled at, or even worse, giving or getting the silent treatment?

When you're out with your spouse or lover does your blood boil because you notice sneaky glances being made at someone attractive (and it's definitely not you)?

Do you find that love or the lack of it makes you implode with all kinds of negative emotions like self-pity, resentment, regret, and hostility that are making you feel even more awful?

Well, join the group.

We've *all* been there in experiencing some or all of the above, (and the few who'll say they haven't are rarer than the almost-extinct snail darter, and maybe they're not telling the absolute snow-white truth, either—at some point, even if it was in high school, *somebody* rejected them). I don't care if you're the most gorgeous female alive, reeking with sex appeal and money, or the most stupendous-looking male with POWER written all over you, chances are you've lost a love somewhere along the way.

I know it's sometimes tough to *admit* having failed at love, but that doesn't make you a failure—it only makes you human. One of the handsomest guys I've ever met, who also happens to have a sensational personality, is in the music business and has lots of bread and success and charm—but he was torching for the longest time over his wife, who'd left him for someone else. And the funny part is that when they first met, *she* was in the pits over being dumped by a TV star and my friend helped put her back together. And so it goes . . .

Look at Bob Evans—could you find a man with more going for him? He's got great looks and super-wealth, is a power in the film industry, yet he was disconsolate over Ali MacGraw leaving him for Steve McQueen. It took years for him to get over this, and there are those in Hollywood who say he'll *never* get over it. And then Ali MacGraw left Steve McQueen, etc., etc., etc.

I've been there . . . you've been there . . . and even though knowing we've all been there helps a little (like AA helps alcoholics and Gaminon helps gamblers), it's still a personal time of hell while you're

going through the trauma of a breakup. I know
what the pain is and I honestly wouldn't wish it on
anyone. It causes you to lose weight, (get fat?), look
awful, get sick, feel worthless and/or just plain
want to die.

Because none of us is exempt from love, we all
need to learn how to cope when problems arise.
And this book will help you to cope in a very positive way—by energizing you physically, mentally
and emotionally. It will turn your body, mind and
feelings around so that love energy will flow
through every cell of your body (ummm), and every
feeling surging through you (double ummm), and
you'll love and be loved as you never have before.
I've written it in three parts—how to love and get
to know your self, how to love and get to know your
Giant Self, and how to love and get to know someone else.

There has been a lot said about liking your self
and being a friend to your self, but I'm not talking
about just liking your self, I'm convinced you must
love your self—really care for and consider your
self, not just a friend but the most important person
in your whole life. Now that doesn't mean making
goo-goo eyes at your self at the mirror (narcissism
is really a form of self-hate, not self-love). At first
you don't have to love *all* of your self—you can
begin by finding just one little quality that's lovable
and trying to strengthen that. The stronger it gets,
the more you'll care for yourself. And of course, in
order to love your self, you'll have to get rid of any
terrible, mean things about your self—you just can't
love your self if you're an awful person, so you'll

have to start acting nicer to your self and others. So when you start to love your self, *everyone* benefits, you and the whole world.

Now you may not be familiar with your Giant Self, but by the time you finish this book you will be. Your Giant Self is the part of you that you'll love the very best because it's the part of you (your subconscious or super-conscious depending on your viewpoint) that will lead you to everything you want once you learn to trust it. Trust is the most important part of loving your self, your Giant Self or someone else, and once you really begin to trust your Giant Self, you'll be surprised to see what happens. I'll give you definite, positive things to do to earn this trust. They're not difficult—in fact, they're fun—and the results are exciting.

The third part of the book deals with loving other people, things you can do to become a great lover and things you can do to vastly improve your sex life (being a great lover and a great sex-partner are two different things), and ways to find and hold love with a special person.

The first book I wrote I dedicated *"To Love Which Is God,"* my *"Energy"* book I dedicated *"To Love Which Is God Which Is Love,"* and this book *"To Love Which Is God Which Is Love Which Is God."* So you don't think I'm crackers, I'd like to explain why I did this. When I was a very little kid in the first grade (I went twelve years to a religious school), I was given a catechism (a book about religion) and told to memorize it. All of us kids had to, and every day we'd have to recite different parts. The first question in the book was "Who is God?" And the answer was "God is Love." Well, to a six-year-old that means about as much as memorizing Einstein's Theory of Relativity ($E = MC^2$) and reciting it, not knowing or understanding what any of it means. A six-year-old mind grasps God as a very kindly old man with a long white beard sitting somewhere up in the heavens—someone you prayed to and got angry with when He didn't give you what you wanted and were very happy with when He did give you what you wanted. Certainly "God is Love" meant nothing. All through grammar and high schools we were still taught this and it still meant nothing. But over the period of years I sometimes mused over how God could be Love and what in the world did that mean? That the Old Man with the white beard was loving? Then, one day, several years ago, the light bulb went on in my head and I thought: "You dummy, God isn't Love, some passive mental state. But Love, the *act* of love and *acting* loving and *doing* kind things—that's what God is." It really blew the top of my head off. I thought about it for days. If everybody *acted* love instead of thinking about it or talking about it, if everybody literally *acted* lovingly, then there couldn't (not shouldn't or wouldn't, but *couldn't*) be any crime or hatred or yelling or anger or jealousy.

Now lots of people have been loving to me and have helped me immensely to become a more loving person, and this has made me a lot happier and my life a lot more fun. And if I can help you just a little bit to love your self more than you did, or to be able to express love and to become more loving to everyone around you, that will help *me* to become more loving, because we're all connected and when I'm more loving it touches you and when you're more loving it touches me. We're all in this together, and love makes us know we're all one.

"Hell is the condition of those who cannot love."

FEDOR DOSTOEVSKY

"Heaven is the condition of those who *can* love."

NAURA HAYDEN

ISLE OF ME

¶1

Pleasuring Me
Physically

I want all the pleasure I can get. And why not? Who deserves it more than I? Haven't I been watching out for myself since I was a little kid? Oh, sure, I had parents and teachers watching over me too, but didn't I make lots of decisions for myself? And then when I hit eighteen, didn't I take over full responsibility for my own life? And haven't I worked hard making a living and making relationships, and trying to make myself a better person at the same time? Haven't I had my "ups" which were fun and exciting, and my "downs" which were awful and full of pain? But I lived through both of them and I'm still working hard making a living and making relationships and trying to make myself a better person. So who better to pleasure than me?

Now by pleasuring me I don't mean stuffing chocolate cream puffs in my mouth or going to orgies.
There's nothing wrong with chocolate cream puffs
or orgies, but they're just not for me. In the first
place, gooey desserts are bad for me and make me fat
and mess up my body chemistry, which makes me
tense, so I don't *want* a banana split with three different kinds of ice cream and syrup (you can tell my
sense memory hasn't faded, right?). And orgies are
for people who are afraid of intimacy with one person, and intimacy is a turn-on for me.

So pleasuring me means doing all the things for
my self that I know will make me feel good without
any bad side effects . . . caring for me in the best
sense of the word.

Now what's the best way to care for our selves, to
really take care of all the things that will make each
one of us happier? The first thing you have to do is
find out all about your self, what makes you tick,
and where better to start than with the bod? You
cannot be mentally and emotionally happy if your
body's a wreck, or just not in good shape. It's impossible to be mentally alert and sharp, and emotionally
a warm, loving person if your body's screaming out
with tension or in the pits of depression or nervous
and full of anxiety. Almost always a physically sick
person is self-centered or selfish, and how can he or
she help it? If you're in physical pain, all you can
think about is your physical pain and how to get rid
of it. The same with anxiety (mental pain), which
comes from tension, and depression (emotional
pain), which comes from a lack of energy caused by

exhaution as an after-effect of tension.

People are so used to feeling tense that they think it's a natural way of life—that that's the way they're *supposed* to feel. Only after they've gotten rid of tension do they realize how awful they *used* to feel and how *un*natural it is to feel that awful. The natural way to feel is relaxed yet full of energy, waking up in the morning looking to conquer the world with enthusiasm. That's what life is *supposed* to be like. But most people don't feel that good, and I sure didn't used to, either. I used to be full of tension and anxiety, then I'd fall into the pits of depression. I used to think my fears and depressions were all mental, so I tried everything—yoga, psychologists, psychiatrists, meditation—but let me tell you, you can meditate for six months or see a shrink for three years, and if your body's screaming out with tension, nothing mental is going to help. But once you get your body in great shape, you'll probably find you don't need el shrinko (or if you do, you'll find that with a relaxed body, your mind will also be more relaxed and you'll be able to solve your emotional problems a lot faster), and the meditation you might still want to do will be the icing on the cake. When your body is feeling super good, you'll start thinking more clearly than you ever did before— you'll find you don't get confused anymore. And you'll be amazed at how your personal relationships will improve. People will find you more relaxed and more loving—because when you're relaxed you don't yell at your kids or pick fights with your spouse or roomie.

And your sex life will be reborn. Even if it's good

now, it'll become *great*. And if it's awful now, it will still become great. After I tell you how to get your body in fantastic shape physically, I'm going to tell you how to have an incredible sex life, how to really pleasure your self.

So as you read on about how you can change your body chemistry and feel terrific and less tense and more relaxed, remember that this is all leading to a life full of pleasure—physical-sensuality pleasure, mental-stimulus pleasure, and emotional-security pleasure. After you've read about how to change your body chemistry, you'll read about how to pleasure this newfound beautiful body.

So the very first step is to get rid of physical tension, and I've found the all-time best way to do this. If this sounds miraculous, in my life it was. Only a person who's felt as low and really awful as I used to feel can understand why I consider the great change that happened to me several years ago a miracle. Anything that could change my life so drastically, that could make me feel *this* good every day, *is* a miracle.

Everyone who read my "Energy" book knows how I changed my life, but I'd like to tell my new readers about how it happened. Before my great discovery, I was a wreck on my ten cups of coffee, my pack a day (at least) of cigarettes, and so many sweets I'm astounded I was able to function at all (and that's all I was doing—functioning, not enjoying life at all). I was tense and anxious all the time. Every day I smoked and drank coffee and ate candy and cakes to whip myself into action. Then I'd have a martini to relax at the end of the day, then coffee, cigs and sweets after dinner to push myself again, and then to bed where I slept poorly with many nightmares, and the next morning the same routine all over again. My sex life was awful. I had lots of fellas but I was so tense I couldn't enjoy sex. Finally, I had a physical collapse where I literally couldn't walk across the room—I had *no* energy—my body had just given out. They took me to the hospital and thought I had mono or a kidney disease—and mind you I was very young, in my early twenties. While I was in the hospital I met Adelle Davis via her books and saw myself in her case stories. She said that canker sores were from tension created by a lack of the B vitamins (and I'd had canker sores since I was a little kid), and that yeast is the most concentrated source of all the B vites in any food—so that's when I invented my Dynamite Milkshake. Not only did the canker sores go away but the tension just sort of drained out of my body. I could feel it leaving and a wonderful sense of well-being take over, and that well-being transferred itself to my romantic life. Sex became a voluptuous experience when I slowed down and relaxed and got to know my body and all its beautiful feelings.

I wrote about my Dynamite Milkshake in my "Energy" book, but now you don't have to make it yourself—you can buy it ready-made at health stores (it costs less ready-made than buying the separate ingredients and mixing them yourself), and it tastes *great* (I worked months perfecting the formula so that it not only would make you feel sensational but would also taste terrific). You can buy a can for your kitchen or one-serving packets for traveling or to put in your purse or pocket for lunch.

While writing this book I got my editor a can of the ready-made, and now she drinks it every day for breakfast and says it makes her whole body feel more alive. I believe in it so much, I'm so positive that it'll help every person who drinks it every day, that I decided not to make any money *ever* on the sale of it. It's the least I can do to show how grateful I am for feeling so sensational now. I want other people to feel as good as I do every day because that's what life is all about—feeling good and sharing the goodness.

All the money that would have come to me from the sale of the Dynamite Milkshake, every penny, is going into a foundation that is giving free Dynamite Milkshakes to people who can't afford it or who wouldn't be able to get it. I want to give it to every prison I can get it into because I truly believe that some people commit crimes because of nutritional deficiencies that lead to tension. The same way some people drink to escape tension and some gamble to release tension and some fight with their mates and kids and friends as a result of tension, some people who have chemically imbalanced bodies and serious nutritional deficiencies commit crimes because of the tension.

Nutritional deficiencies also lead to depression which is the other side of tension. I've found in my life that when I used to be depressed, anger got rid of the awful depression so I would unconsciously think of things which would make me angry. *You can't be depressed and angry at the same time.* Of course the anger causes tension, and some depressed people turn the anger inward, on themselves, and are self-destructive. They eat too much, drink and smoke too much and some of them commit suicide, while others take out their anger on people around them, and either scream and yell a lot, hit their kids, or get into fights. And of course those with chemically imbalanced bodies, who are more seriously nutritionally deficient, may escape their terrible depression with an anger so ferocious that they can only relieve that tension with a robbery, rape or murder.

So when a person gets rid of tension and depression, he or she will start thinking more clearly and better than ever before, and start being a more loving person than ever before.

I also want to get disadvantaged, malnourished kids to drink the shake. I wish to God I had been given it when I was a kid—I wouldn't have had all those horrible problems I had while I was growing up (canker sores in my mouth almost constantly since childhood, neuralgia attacks in my face when I was a teenager, bad teenage skin, terrible tension which made my life miserable, just to name a few). Maybe if enough kids drink it they'll be rid of a lot of problems that they and those around them have to suffer with. And wouldn't it be terrific if older people, who often suffer from calcium deficiency, would take it, and maybe stop falling apart and breaking bones and losing teeth and ending up in wheelchairs, passive and unhappy, but instead feeling really sensational and keeping active and happy all the way? The milkshake totally changed my life, and it thrills me to be able to help other people to feel as good as I feel now.

Again, let me make this clear—I am not now making one penny (nor have I ever made, nor will I ever make any money) on my Dynamite Milkshake. Every cent is spent giving free milkshakes to those people who wouldn't be able to get it otherwise—people in prisons, mental institutes, old people's homes and other institutions—who I feel could be benefitted enormously by getting something this potent in their bodies that could change their physical, mental and emotional lives.

My very dear friend Dr. Neil Solomon, who has written several best-sellers and now writes a syndicated column in newspapers all over the U.S., believes as much as I do in the Dynamite Milkshake and has helped me get it into the Maryland State Penitentiary through his friend and now mine, Warden George Collins, and I hope eventually to get it into many more. I know the results at the prisons so far have been very positive. When I visited one prison, the men told me how much better they felt after taking the Dynamite Milkshake, how much less depressed and more energetic. One of the prisoners, who is in for twenty-five years to life, wrote me a beautiful letter about how much less tense he felt and how he was beginning to have some hope for the future, which was so totally bleak before.

For those who'd still rather make the milkshake themselves than buy it ready-made, I have listed the recipe and a list of vites to take with it at the end of this book in a special appendix called "Vites and the Dynamite Milkshake."

I drink an enormous amount of milk (at least a quart a day) and I love it. But for those of you who up to now haven't been able to digest milk there's now a tablet available at health stores containing the enzyme needed to digest lactose, so now you can drink as much milk as you like.

Another very important thing I take every day is dolomite, which consists of calcium and magnesium —both super-important to your nerves, and it also keeps your bones strong. You know how you always hear about elderly people breaking their legs or hip bones? And they always say that they tripped and fell? Well, it's been found that these peoples' bones are so brittle and porous from a lack of calcium that they have a spontaneous fracture just from their body weight. They *think* that they tripped and fell, but the truth is that the leg bone snapped spontaneously from body weight and they fell as a result of the break. It's incredible how few older people drink milk or get calcium in any other form (in America, milk is the best food source of calcium), so dolomite is terribly important to take every day for young and old. I've had a few people ask me if it's safe to take lots of dolomite, and I've told them that I take a minimum of thirty and sometimes up to sixty tablets a day (I swallow them ten at a time— they're one of the reasons my throat's relaxed so much).

Now there are lots of terrific doctors in the world, but it's up to each one of us to learn as much as we can about keeping our bodies healthy. Most medical schools teach doctors how to cure people with drugs once they're already sick, but not how to keep you from getting sick. They're trained in sickness and not in health. In old China, doctors were paid a small stipend monthly as long as the person was well, and were paid nothing when the person got sick. I have found that the younger, hipper doctors are really getting into preventive medicine, and I've met many terrific doctors who are already into it. Some of them have written some fine books. Dr. Harold Rosenberg wrote *The Doctor's Book of Vitamin Therapy*, Dr. Henry Newbold wrote *Mega-Nutrients*, Dr. Richard Brennan wrote *Nutrigenetics* and Dr. Richard Passwater (a Ph.D.) wrote *Super Nutrition for Healthy Hearts*. Dr. Robert Atkins has written several fine books, as has Dr. Neil Solomon. Count yourself lucky if your doctor knows about vitamins and vitamin therapy. Hopefully all doctors will sometime in the future be trained in this. Every year a few more medical schools put nutrition in their curriculum. But in the meantime, if your doctor doesn't know, it's up to you to cure your self. Now naturally I'm not talking about a serious illness or not having an operation if three doctors tell you that you need one. I'm talking about learning how to take your own blood pressure (you can now order a sphygmomenometer through mail order ads found in lots of magazines), reading up on gout or kidney stones or arthritis (read Adelle Davis' *Let's Get Well*), subscribing to *Prevention* and *Let's Live* magazines and reading about all the newest discoveries in preventive medicine.

In Dr. Harold Rosenberg's terrific book, *The Doctor's Book on Vitamin Therapy*, he says:

Dolomite is a naturally occurring inexpensive substance that contains calcium and magnesium in
roughly the best proportion, approximately two to
one. Therefore, we recommend that you add dolomite
supplements to your dietary regimen. These can be
found in many health shops at very low cost. Enough
should be taken for a total of at least one or two grams
(1,000–2,000 mg) of calcium daily. The proper amount
of magnesium will then accompany the calcium.

*There is no possibility whatever of any danger due to an
excess of dolomite.* Quite the contrary. While some minerals (iodine, zinc) may cause problems when taken to
excess, the calcium-magnesium combination found in
dolomite is safe in any conceivable supplement quan-
tity. In fact, this additional supplementation is especially important for the elderly, who may be having
bone weaknesses, and also for the many adults whose
digestive systems will not accommodate milk and who
do not eat much cheese. Calcium is often poorly absorbed, so amounts even up to four or five gm (4,000
to 5,000 mg) may at times be helpful.

I learned how calcium strengthens your nervous
system in a roundabout way. A few years ago I read
Psycho-Cybernetics by my dear friend, the late Dr.
Maxwell Maltz, and one thing that stood out in my
mind was his report on tests made with sodium
pentothal, or truth serum. The reason it works is
that it completely relaxes the body—I mean *totally;*
every muscle is relaxed. And they found that a person cannot experience a negative emotion when he
or she is totally relaxed. You can't feel envy or anger
or hate or fear when you're completely relaxed.
Well, one day I found myself in Rio de Janeiro very

nervous about appearing on a TV show, the biggest in Brazil, with a rating of almost 50,000,000 people watching. The thing that made me most nervous was that the whole show was built around me and my acting appearances on U.S. TV shows (like *Bonanza* and *Gunsmoke*)—one hour of me singing and dancing and trying to communicate with the TV host in my phumphering Portuguese. As the date drew nearer I became more and more nervous. Then, all of a sudden, the truth-serum story popped into my head. If you couldn't help but tell the truth while you were so relaxed, because you couldn't be afraid or feel any negative emotion while taking a relaxant like sodium pentothal—and I knew calcium was also a relaxant, why wouldn't the *same* thing work with calcium? So I went out and bought some extra calcium pills and started taking them the afternoon of rehearsal. By one-half hour before show time that night, I was fairly cool. But as the minutes ticked by getting closer to a live performance, the tension slowly mounted. I was socking away that calcium like peanuts, and the amazing thing was I could literally feel the tension ebb with every pill. Now the closer to starting the TV show we got, the more apprehensive I would have been getting, but the pills worked and by showtime I was really relaxed and went out and did my thing—and I've done it many times since.

As more and more doctors get into preventive medicine and learn about nutrition and vites, they're beginning to use calcium as a pain reliever. And I've heard of some dentists who are using injections of calcium instead of novocaine to deaden pain.

All I can tell you is—try it. Wait till you have a particularly stressful day with one really important appointment that's making you a nervous wreck and filling you with tension. Then, on that awful day, begin taking dolomite. You can either mix the powdered dolomite (one level teaspoon = roughly ten pills) in milk or juice, or you can pop the pills. Ten dolomite pills are about equal to the amount of calcium in one quart of milk—plus you're getting the added benefit of magnesium, which is found in dolomite with calcium in the right ratio needed by the body. Start with ten tablets (or one teaspoon), and half an hour later take ten more or another teaspoon, until you start feeling the terrible tension ebbing out of your body. You'll know when you've had enough when you start to feel relaxed and the anxiety and fear have left you.

Remember, you can't experience a negative emotion when your body is completely relaxed. And who needs any negative emotion? Not me—I want to make room for all the positive things in life I want.

Lots of people when they get tense take "downers"—tranquilizers, sleeping pills, booze, etc. Sure it relaxes you temporarily—but it also screws up every area of your body, particularly your breathing. Your diaphragm at the base of your lungs is a muscle, which pushes the stale air out and allows fresh air to rush in and fill all the cavities. When "downers" become a habit you constrict your diaphragm. When Elvis Presley started using drugs heavily his breathing was affected—so much so that he had a hard time singing, and his performances got badly panned by the critics and audiences. Whatever demons inside Elvis drove him to drugs, we may never know, but we do know that drugs destroyed Elvis—ruined his career and finally killed him at the age of forty-two.

Because alcohol is accepted by society, we tend not to think of it as a drug, but it's as much a "mind-bender" as speed, heroin, or cocaine. People are addicted to alcohol as much as they are to other drugs, and it's really a bigger problem because it is so accepted and so many people use it. A hundred years ago Stephen Foster died a drunk because he couldn't face the pain of not being accepted as a songwriter. Jimi Hendrix and Janis Joplin o.d.'d on drugs and booze—they couldn't believe they were happening They seemed to be sure of themselves only when they were singing. Dana Andrews, who was so great with Gene Tierney in *Laura* (Otto Preminger's sensational picture), almost ruined his career with alcohol. The pressures of success almost got him.

So many show-biz personalities have saved themselves through Alcoholics Anonymous—Mercedes McCambridge and Dick Van Dyke to name just two. But many others ruined their lives with alcohol. Look at John Barrymore and his daughter Diana (just as diabetes or hypoglycemia runs in families, a weakness for alcohol does too—these are chemical imbalances, and we are chemically a result of our mothers' and fathers' chemical balances or

imbalances). Jim Thorpe, considered by many to be
the greatest athlete of the century—an Olympic de-
cathlon champion, a football immortal and a base-
ball player—died from drinking and Marilyn
Monroe, America's sex symbol, couldn't face reality
without alcohol as a crutch. During the day she
drank and at night she couldn't go to sleep without
sleeping pills.

What a pity that these exceptional people had to
use drugs to get through the days and nights. And
what a waste—you can't mistreat your body without your body rebelling. The tensions get worse and
the depressions deepen when the effects of booze
and other drugs wear off. So you constantly need
heavier doses until finally you're so hooked you
can't function anymore.

The answer is—find another way to cope with
life's stresses. We all have problems, every last one
of us, and we all find different ways to cope. My way
is my milkshake and vites—and believe me, they
really work. Your body will feel better and you
won't get the letdown you get with stimulants.
You'll just feel better all day long.

You cannot mistreat your body over a period of
time and not pay with the results. "Downers"—
booze, pillls, etc.—are used by desperate people in
search of peace. They're tortured by anxiety, tensions, fear, insecurity, etc. I know, because I was
there. I've used pills to calm myself (before I discovered my Dynamite Milkshake and vites) and a few
drinks to get rid of anxiety. I was there—I know
how awful it is to be dependent on these drugs.
Fortunately for me, I would get a pill "hangover"

the next day, and on booze, even though I would have a great time the night I was drinking, the next day I would be so sick I'd have to stay in bed the whole day. You'd think the first time that happened I would have stopped the martinis before din-din, but it took a long time for me to realize I was ruining my life wasting days in bed when I could have been doing something constructive. Not until I invented my Dynamite Milkshake was I able to feel so truly great I didn't *need* a drink to feel better. I just phased out booze because I found I was "up" all the time, and yet relaxed and not tense and anxious after my shake and vites. If you're feeling *great* you obviously don't need to feel greater. It's those of us who feel awful physically, mentally and emotionally (and they *do* go together) who need to stimulate ourselves or dull our anxieties. When we feel physically great and rarin' to go, it's almost impossible to be depressed mentally or emotionally, unless, of course, a major tragedy befalls us. The death of a loved one is heart-rending no matter how well we feel physically, but when our bodies are in great shape, it's easier for us to endure the tragedy and go on living. I'd like to tell you a story that really made me feel terrific, about how my milkshake helped someone cope with a terrible loss.

Recently I was in Los Angeles promoting my new record single, "Equal Time" (giving Paul Simon what-for because of his "Fifty Ways to Leave Your Lover," and changing his "Slip out the back, Jack" to my "Hop in a train, Jane"), and I sang it on *AM-LA*, a local TV show hosted by that fabulous Regis Philbin, one of the funniest men I've ever met. After I sang my song, Regis asked me how my Dynamite Milkshake was doing and I said great. Then he asked me if I knew Georgia Rosenbloom, and I said no, but that I'd heard about her and how she took over the Los Angeles Rams after her husband, Carroll Rosenbloom, died. Regis said that Gladys told him she couldn't have gotten through the trauma of her husband's untimely death without my Dynamite Milkshake—that taking it every day pulled her through. He said this on the air and it really made me feel as if all my work was worthwhile. It's amazing what a little positive feedback will do.

Do you have any idea how many millions of people are taking sleeping pills and tranquilizers every day and night? If they knew about dolomite they could save lots of money and their bodies, too, because dolomite is good for you and drugs ain't. Dolomite is both a relaxant and tranquilizer in a natural form and it'll help you to sleep. I've been using it for years and I sleep like a baby (a healthy baby!).

You can tell how much dolomite you need by how you feel—take ten pills with yogurt or milk or juice and see how you feel. If you start really relaxing, then ten is enough, but if you still feel uptight, take ten more—and continue till you feel super-relaxed. People have asked me how much to take and I tell them everyone is different chemically and has different needs. I personally need a lot. My last long-term relationship (I'll be tactful and not mention with whom, to protect the guilty) was so traumatic and stressful that for a long time I was taking at least eighty dolomites and sometimes more every day, and the day we split up (would you believe the *very day?*) I just automatically cut back to thirty a day (don't forget, you don't have to take the pills, you can take the powder and mix it with milk or juice or whatever).

Once you've got your body in great shape by substituting healthy energizers like the Dynamite Milkshake, vites and dolomite for the unhealthy stimulants like pills and booze and coffee and junk food, you'll want to put all that newfound energy to work to help keep yourself fit, and the best way I know to do that is through exercise and/or active sports. That's how the celebrities keep in shape— Farrah Fawcett plays tennis, as does Cheryl Tiegs, Dino (Dean Paul) Martin, Ali MacGraw, Dustin Hoffman and me, among millions of others. Dean Martin and Bob Hope play golf. Swimming, touch football, volley ball, handball, bike-riding and roller skating are great exercise and even greater fun!

Exercise is even more fun if you have someone to do it with you. Frank Gifford, who was an all-American football player at USC, a big star with the New York Giants and is now one of the top sportscasters in the country on network TV, jogs with his wife, Astrid, every day—she runs three miles and he runs two (he says that's because she's in better shape than he is). Astrid also teaches Aerobic dancing, which is an exercise dance using every muscle in the body. They also ski, play tennis and paddle tennis, swim, and ride bikes together in the country, and sometimes in Central Park. Frank is also a great believer in vitamins, and takes them every day. He weighs exactly the same today as he did in high school and is the same size.

Disco dancing is sensational for your body, and you don't need Studio 54 or Ipanema or any other fantastic disco palace to do it. All you need is a record or tape player or a cassette and a little privacy in your own room. And you don't really even need the privacy. If you've learned a few good steps and know you're good, you won't care who's watching. The beat of the music is so powerful that if you're not all tensed up you can't help but move, even just to tap your feet. If you're a little shy, be alone and just move to the music—march, jump, swing your arms, move with your pelvis. Just try one disco record (the Bee Gees are my favorite), and see if you can sit or stand still while the music is blasting. Rock is very primitive, with the strong bass and drum beats (millenia ago our ancestors were jumping to a tom-tom beat). It's the beat of life, like your heartbeat, and you can't help but respond to it.

Sometimes I put on a couple of my favorite albums and dance for half an hour by myself—by the last tune I'm pooped, but I feel great. It's like running a mile or two except for me it's more fun—not that jogging isn't. I do that every day in my house for about two or three minutes. I start in my bedroom on my jogger, then when I get bored, I run into my study and run in place while I look at a few paintings on the wall (they're all pastelly outdoor scenes of beaches and parks and flowers), and then I end up in my bedroom again feeling super-good. I guess it's better if you can run outdoors but I don't get much of a chance, so I substitute inside and it's probably the same distance either way (two minutes on the jogger is equivalent to running fifteen minutes on a flat surface). But the disco dancing is to rhythm and my body really responds to music. Anything that turns you on to charge up your battery is good. Bike riding is great—every weekend I see hundreds of people riding toward Central Park (and other hundreds cruising up Park Avenue or across Fifty-seventh Street), and they spend hours winding along the terrific bike paths.

If a person is fat, it's bad enough to look awful and blubbery, but that's not the worst part. It's so unhealthy. I know it's been said before, but honestly, try to imagine lugging around a 25-pound weight or a 50-pound golf case sixteen hours a day. A healthy person *can't* be fat. The fat is showing you there's a chemical imbalance in the body—it's a symptom that the body isn't functioning the way it should. Once you understand this, it's just a matter of balancing out your body's chemistry—of balancing the chemical imbalance. A good way to start is with the Dynamite Milkshake and vites.

Once your body cells get a slug of these powerful ingredients, you'll start shedding pounds gradually and painlessly. I've gotten thousands of letters from people attesting to this, and many of my friends have lost a lot of weight and are slim for the first time in years. Everyone says the milkshake fills you up and takes away your appetite. After the milkshake for breakfast, you're not that hungry at lunch (some people aren't very hungry at all) and mid-afternoon you won't get that usual letdown that urges you to have a Coke or candy bar to pep you up (they're only temporary "uppers"—a few minutes later you're lower than before you ate them, so you need another, and so on in a vicious circle). At dinner you won't be ravenously hungry so you'll eat less compulsively, meaning you'll be calmer and sharper about what not to eat and you'll be able to use your head and choose better food, and less food.

Warren Beatty is very much into self-improvement via vites and exercise. He was the captain of his high school football team back in Arlington, Virginia, and he works hard to keep his body in the same great shape it was in then. He doesn't drink or smoke, stays away from all drugs, and eats only foods which he knows will build health.

Mitzi Gaynor also takes great care of herself and it sure shows. She's got a gorgeous face and body, but she works at it (you have to work at it to keep your muscles in shape—everything in life is an effect of a cause; exercise tones muscles and keeps your body firm and supple, and no exercise allows your muscles to atrophy and your body to sag and droop). Mitzi jogs and works out at her dance class every day and doesn't put any junk into her mouth —she eats wisely and well, and takes her vites every day.

Clay Cole is a writer and producer and one of the warmest, wittiest TV personalities I've ever worked with. We met when I first came to New York and he hosted *The Clay Cole Show* which was terrific and into contemporary music. Now he's been co-hosting the *AM-New York* TV show with that fantastic Janet Langhart (whom I originally met in Boston when she co-hosted *Good Day* with John Willis, whom I originally met when he co-hosted *Panorama* in Washington, D.C., which was produced by Sheila Weidenfeld who quit to become Betty Ford's press secretary and then wrote a book about those experiences, and we co-guested in Detroit on *Kelly and Company* with John Kelly and Marilyn Turner . . . the motto of all this is: write a book and see the world and make lots of friends). Anyway, Clay and Janet are some team—really fun to work with. Clay tells everyone the Dynamite Milkshake has changed his life—he says he doesn't need coffee anymore and feels terrific, and Janet takes it every morning and says it makes her feel good and energetic.

Otto Preminger walks all over New York every day and generally only takes a cab when it rains. He's terribly energetic and is in terrific shape because of all the exercise of walking. To try to control his weight he goes without dinner several nights a week and says it doesn't bother him at all. He eats well at breakfast and lunch and the no-dinner is his way of trying to keep trim and fit. Otto also drinks the Dynamite Milkshake every morning for breakfast, as do Monique Van Vooren, Arlene Dahl, Warren Avis, Regis Philbin, and lots of other energy-seeking people. Arlene, Monique and Janet are gorgeous females, and by putting this in their bodies every day, they're going to *stay* gorgeous.

One of the greatest pleasures of life is sex. Sex is a body function, like eating, drinking, sleeping or walking. Every person in the world has the life force of a sex drive, within him or her, everyone without exception. Some people have stronger sex drives and some weaker, but they all exist. Not everyone expresses or uses it, though. Sex, like everything else, is composed of the physical, mental and emotional, and sometimes, when one of these components gets out of kilter, we stop getting pleasure from sex, or even experiencing sex at all. Repressed sex is tension (repressed *anything* is tension—repression means that there is something that wants to be expressed which we are holding back, or stopping, through tension, from expression. But because a person says he or she is asexual, or non-sexual, or even anti-sexual doesn't mean the sex drive isn't there. Just as everyone has an appetite for food, everyone has an appetite for sex. Now some people go on fasts and live for days without food, but they can go only so long without it. A person will not die without sex, but the tension brought on by repressing the sex drive and denying its existence can cause many illnesses—physical, mental and emotional. If you don't move your body, it won't die right away but the muscles will atrophy and the organs will not function as well as when they are used and exercised. So it is with sex: a healthy body, a really healthy body, will desire a sexual release. We were all born with this drive, and denying it will never make it go away. There are healthy people who sublimate their sexual desires, but with some damage to themselves physically, mentally or emotionally. Nature always wins out.

Which is not to say there can't be too much of a good thing. Just as you can't fast forever, you also can't daily glut your body with food to the bursting point and live a long and healthy life. In the same way, you can't totally abstain from sex or constantly glut your body with too much—too much or too little of anything isn't healthy.

Now to the B vites and the Dynamite Milkshake and how they affect sex. I believe that each one of us, men and women both, has experienced temporary impotence (for the luckier ones it's been temporary). Which one of us hasn't tried to make love and felt nothing? Unless it's a physiological problem—disease or blockage—male and female impotence (in women it's sometimes called frigidity) *is* caused by tension. Tension constricts the blood vessels—the blood vessels engorging with blood causes sexual excitement—and restricts the circulation. So if you're a heavy smoker, which constricts the blood vessels, or if you're a big coffee drinker, which causes tension and constricts the blood vessels, or a heavy sugar eater, which uses up all the B vites and causes tensions throughout your body, don't be surprised if your sex life isn't groovy—and don't complain. If you *really* miss a great sex life and the feeling of fulfillment and contentment that go with it, all you have to do is determine to stop the junk and put in something to replace them which will give you more and better and longer-lasting energy than they did.

Now some doctors have told me if I had given up coffee, sugar and cigarettes, I could have done all the good things to my body without the vites and the milkshake. But what they don't realize (and I've tried to tell them but they don't understand) is that I literally *couldn't have functioned* without the stimulants. I wouldn't have been able to move, to get dressed, to go to work without the caffeine pushing me and the nicotine stimulating me and the sugar driving me. All drugs work the same: you start with a small amount and work your way up to a dependence on a larger amount. I was dependent on these "uppers," and had I been able to get rid of them I would have, but I was not able to get my body going without them. The milkshake gave me natural energy (an "upper" without a "downer" following, like the stimulants—the shake keeps you going *all day*) so I found I didn't need ten cups of coffee, I only needed eight, then a few weeks later six, and so on till I found I didn't need *any* coffee—the shake and vites were doing it all. And the depressions that used to follow the anxiety attacks were all gone too. My depressions used to last for days; I used to feel that life wasn't worth living, I was so down. The shakes and vites kept me "up" and I haven't had a depression since.

Repressed sex is tension and the obvious way to release the tension is to make love. But conversely, tension also makes for repressed sex. Your body may be screaming out with tension from all those candy bars and cups of coffee and you've got the weight of the world on your shoulders with all kinds of mental problems (how in the world can I pay the rent—I can't even afford a peanut butter sandwich?) or emotional worrying (why does she want to move out, be independent and "find her own identity"?—God knows I was very good to her and how can I get her back?). So your body must be tension-free to truly enjoy sex, and we already know how to do that (for those opening the book in the middle, we cut out junk and sugar and coffee and put in the Dynamite Milkshake and vites and with the newfound energy we jog and walk a lot), and when we do it we soon discover that most probably the so-called frigidity or impotence was a direct result of physical tension.

Many of the tensions caused by mental problems will automatically disappear when the old bod is in great shape, and even if they don't disappear you'll be astounded at how you'll be able to objectively figure out and analyze the problems and come up with workable solutions (I can't pay the rent or afford a peanut-butter sandwich so I'm obviously doing something wrong—meantime I'll borrow some money to tide me over and I'll intelligently go about getting a job that I like and that pays well). And when your body relaxes, you'll find your emotional anxieties will lessen and you'll be able to calmly figure out what went wrong with your marriage or relationship (now that I think about it, I guess I could have made her feel more important, and maybe I did tend to put her down in little ways —now that I'm feeling better about myself I can show her how important she really is to me and try to convince her that we're much stronger as a team than we are singly).

If you're into some negative emotions (like anger or hostility) and you're really mad, your muscles get rigid and you can't have an orgasm.

I again want to talk about the sodium pentothal (truth serum) experiment, and show how we can use the same theory for a terrific sex life. Sodium pentothal so totally relaxes your muscles that you're not afraid to tell the truth, and when the body is totally relaxed it is impossible to feel a negative emotion. You can't experience jealousy, insecurity, fear, hatred, anger or any other negative when you're perfectly relaxed. And of course, when you're terribly tense, you can't experience any positive feeling. So, for all the positive feelings of sex, one must have a deliciously relaxed body, and for a deliciously relaxed body, one must not repress the life force (a.k.a. sex drive). Don't misunderstand me, I am not condoning "free love" (is it ever free?) or wife and husband swapping. I believe in sex with love and, most perfectly, sex with love in marriage. But for those who haven't yet found a partner to share life with (and that's the ultimate fantasy we all have— to love and be loved by someone wonderful who thinks we're wonderful too) and are still seeking, well, they're entitled to love also.

I gave a lot of thought to whether I should write the following advice about sexual satisfaction. The reason I hesitated is a silly, juvenile guilt thing re my mother and some of my other relatives. But I decided how to overcome this with a warning to my mother and all other persons who feel they would be offended with explicit instructions about sex. If you feel you can't handle this kind of thing, then pass the next few paragraphs. If you feel you want to find out why so many women are unsatisfied by so many men and what they can do about it and how they can change it, and why so many men never have what doctors call a *full*, or total, orgasm—and what they can do about it—then read on.

Not long ago I had lunch with a very close friend of mine—she's in her thirties, gorgeous, and holds a top position in one of the film studios—but she's never had an orgasm in the "normal" way (intercourse). I was amazed because I knew she was very active socially (read sexually) and, being unmarried, has lots of boyfriends. She told me that the reason she has so many boyfriends is that she's desperately looking for the one who can satisfy her in this most important way. We talked about it and exchanged ideas and I told her that I used to have this problem but I found the answer.

First of all, some men don't understand the physical, mental or emotional workings of women. Not to say that most men aren't sensational, it's just that lots of them are just not into sensitivity (just as lots of women aren't into football or carburetors). The men who do understand know how to satisfy women, and have happy partners who don't need another man . . . ever. But because many men aren't attuned to women's needs, it's up to women not to be passive and just hope and pray that a man will finally figure out what she wants; even after telling some of them many times, they still don't pick up. Obviously, the more sensitive a man is, and the more ESP he has, the more he will "feel" what a woman wants or doesn't want sexually. Naturally this works both ways (some women are klutzes too), but women seem on the whole to be more sensitive than most men. So, assuming you are an unsatisfied, sexually frustrated woman, who cannot climax during intercourse, you must take control of this situation and end your passivity. I did—and it works.

Pleasuring Me Physically 43

The problem seems to be that most men don't know how to "tease" a woman, and teasing is the most exciting part of sex—wanting the unattainable, then needing it, desperately needing it, then feeling like you'll die if you can't have it; then, finally, attaining it in the most excruciating, pleasure surging feeling that exists. It's like having an itch. The softer you scratch it (teasing), the more excruciating that is until you finally scratch it harder (climax). Or it's sort of like tickling—the softer you tickle, the more excruciating it is (like if you tickle yourself or someone else with a feather); it can drive you mad until you finally scratch it (climax).

A lot of men believe in the "big bang" theory. That is, a lot of men "bang" a woman—and this is just the opposite of teasing. When the base of the male organ (the penis) rams against the female organ (the clitoris), the woman initially feels pain (which makes her tense up), then her whole sexual area loses all feeling. Try it with your arm or leg, try hitting continually for five minutes, and you'll see what I mean. At first it hurts, then it gets sort of numb and loses feeling.

Now if the roles were reversed and the woman were banging or hitting on the man's organ with something hard, he would understand what I mean. But the man is usually in control during intercourse and the woman is usually the receptacle, so the man never gets hit on his penis. If he did, it would hurt and he would get no pleasure from it. When a man bangs, his penis isn't hurt because a woman is soft inside, but when a woman gets banged or hit on the sensitive clitoris, it hurts, tenses her up, and is the turn-off.

It's the teasing of the clitoris and the gentleness-at-first that turns us on. As we slowly build desire for the "unattainable" (it *feels* unattainable—when it's gentle) male organ, that desire eventually becomes overwhelming, and the woman lets the man know with her body that she wants it more and *more* and MORE, till the rockets go off and the universe explodes within her body. This turns the man on even more, to see and hear and feel how he's pleasured his woman, and his climax will be much greater than it ever was when he was unable to arouse her this way.

My girlfriend, who'd never had an orgasm during intercourse, could only be satisfied with oral sex and this in my opinion is only ten percent of sexual satisfaction once you've experienced the soul-shattering sex when two loving bodies are intertwined.

Now for how a woman can control her sexual destiny, can have a climax every time, with a man who hasn't picked up on teasing. You do it with your thighs. When a man comes on too strong and too hard and starts banging, just squeeze your thighs which will clamp around his hips and keep his body from ramming your body and slow him down. Try it—you'll begin to feel as much in charge of your climax as he is of his. And power is an aphrodisiac. Slowly, as he finds out he can't "bang" because you won't *allow* it, he'll start to ease up his attack because he really can't do anything else.

Now when I say squeeze your thighs, I mean *take control*. There are some very strong muscles there that are hardly ever used, and the more you use them, the stronger they get.

Once you have shown a man that you know what you want, and he knows you know what you want, and he begins, gently and lovingly, to move in and out, you can begin to relax and let him take over more. When a woman is physically relaxed, she will be mentally and emotionally relaxed, too. If he gets too rough again, just flex those thigh muscles to signal him to gentle it (not that later, maybe, you won't want it crazy and wild, but you *start* with it teasy). Then, as he gently and lovingly makes love, you can relax and begin to surrender yourself to him, slowly, as he will to you. Sexual surrender is the ultimate in trust—and the ultimate in pleasure. When you're totally open physically, trusting mentally, and vulnerable emotionally, is when the rockets explode. And that's what's so beautiful and sexy and sensual about loving and pleasuring the person you care about.

Since that lunch with my beautiful but unsatisfied girlfriend, I've started asking other women how satisfied they are sexually, and most of them (honestly, *most* of them) say they have problems climaxing. So even though there are hundreds of books and articles about sex, they don't seem to deal with this problem. It's simply a matter of a man becoming aware of a woman's body, and gently teasing "the divine itch" before he scratches it.

Now about a couple of men's problems ("equal time" works both ways). For most men one problem seems to be the most important from the physical standpoint—keeping an erection long enough to pleasure their partners. Now, obviously, if there are psychological problems (like she doesn't turn him on, or she reminds him of his grade school gym teacher), a man must get these mental or emotional problems straightened out before he can function. But I'm talking about purely physical problems, and two things that seem to prevent men from functioning sexually are smoking and drinking.

Of course when we smoke or drink too much (women as well as men) it harms lots of other parts of our bodies, too, like our lungs, our liver, our heart, our skin, etc., but a real barometer of the harm done (and a quicker one) is our sex life. When we smoke, the nicotine constricts our blood vessels (it really makes them a *lot* smaller), and the swelling of the blood vessels is the cause of erection and sexual excitement in both men and women. And the inhaled carbon monoxide reduces the level of blood oxygen and hormone production. When a person is a heavy smoker, the lung capacity is cut way down and that cuts way down on the ability to last during intercourse. Try it. See what happens when you cut out the smokes for a month. If your sex life doesn't pick up considerably (and I mean your ability as a lover), then you can always go back. I know it's difficult to stop, but if I did it, anyone can. It took only a few days before I started feeling better (it took a while longer to stop having dreams about smoking), but my improved sex life made any thoughts about going back to smoking absolutely ludicrous. Who in his or her right mind would trade a voluptuous, juicy, absolutely divine sex life for a few puffs on a few cigarettes? Not me.

One of the wonderful things about life is that things are usually never totally lost. There is usually hope that something can be salvaged. The good news about stopping smoking is that once a person stops, the body is cleared of all the tar and nicotine and assorted gunk in a matter of months. I've spoken to several doctors about this and have been told that people should never feel that because they've been smoking for years that it wouldn't make any difference if they stop smoking—that all the damage has already been done; that's simply not true. Your lungs will go back to their pre-smoking condition a few months after you stop.

Alcoholism is a result of nutritional deficiencies (particularly the B vites), so, because our bodies are malnourished, we crave liquor—which makes our bodies more nutritionally deficient and we become more malnourished and we crave more booze, etc., etc., etc.

So the main thing to do for guys who want to have a super sex life is to cut down the booze, cut out the smokes altogether, and start exercising those gorgeous bodies and getting them in shape. Jogging is a terrific way to begin, even if it's running in place in your pad. Once you see how good you're feeling, you might even graduate to running outside.

Now I'm sure some men smoke and drink too much and still function well, but believe me, they are the exception. And their sexual prowess won't (can't) last. These men start out in life in better shape than the average man, so it just takes the nicotine and booze a little while longer to get to them. But get they will.

Another way for a man to keep an erection is to deliberately hold back his ejaculation. Chinese men are reputed to make the best lovers, and they're trained not to ejaculate but to hold back—both for their own pleasure and for their partner's pleasure. The Chinese culture teaches that the greatest mutual pleasure in sex occurs when the male takes care to stimulate the female's orgasms.

Holding back is something that can be learned. A man can train himself to hold back as long as he can, so when he finally does have an orgasm it will seem like it's going on for a l-o-o-o-o-ng time. It's said that after the ecstasy that comes from a release of prolonged tension, a man will never want to go back to any kind of "quickie" sex again.

It's like everyone can move and walk and dance —maybe not really gracefully, but most of us can move around a dance floor *fairly* well. But when a person takes years and trains his or her body to dance ballet, and really puts some effort forth to become good at it, well, that person may wind up as a prima ballerina or premier danseur in *Swan Lake*. Or like Mikhail Baryshnikov, who was so spectacular in the dance sequences of the film *The Turning Point* (and turned on all the women with his incredibly masculine body). Practice does make perfect, and certainly sex is one of the most important parts of our lives, so why not become a superstar in that area? It just takes time, thought and energy—and what better way to put those three things to work?

A *total* male orgasm, according to many doctors, *never* happens without training, so if you males thought that sex was great before, just wait! A man can teach himself to slow down when he thinks he will come by stopping his thrusting every time he feels ready to come. At first this will no doubt frustrate him and his partner, but that frustration will work *for* them by acting as a "tease" that will heighten the excitement between the two—and the supreme pleasure of the man bringing his partner to climax several times while he experiences the sensual nirvana of teasing himself before he eventually comes. This will boggle his body—not to mention what it will do to his mind.

Have you ever been really hungry and sat down to a sumptuous feast? You can dive right in and quickly gorge yourself with food until you're stuffed and sated. Or you can prolong the pleasure by relaxing, having a glass of wine, and savoring a few appetizers as you await the mouth-watering main course. Your appetite is being teased by the wait, but it's an exciting tease just because you know what's soon in store for you, and in the interim you're mentally building up anticipation and relish for the forthcoming feast.

Which is more pleasure-full? Who in his or her right mind would choose the fast stuffing and gorging over the slow sucking and savoring? Once you've chewed and swallowed, it's all over, but melting-in-the-mouth lasts a long time. And so it is with all our appetites. The connoisseur appreciates life a lot more than the glutton, and certainly receives much more long-lasting pleasure from it.

A man can postpone his orgasm for an hour or several hours or even overnight. He can hold back while he's making love at night and wake up the next morning and start to make love again. (This should be done on a weekend, when you've got *lots* of time.)

When a man trains himself to hold back, he becomes more sensitive physically. Every nerve in every part of his body becomes more acutely sensitive and heightened sensually, so even the slightest touch becomes deliciously erotic. Passion is heightened to such an extent that the whole body is more receptive to stimuli. So there will be lots of hugs and feelies that make you feel even *more* erotic (and loving, I might add).

Why not try it and see if the doctors are right? You'll not only make the woman (women?) in your life a lot happier, you might also be surprised at how much happier and more satisfied you'll be, too.

And for all you enlightened males already into this, I have only two words from all of us women . . .

Thank you.

Can you just imagine what's going to happen when every man gets his body into super-good shape, so it functions the way he wants it to (and the way it's *supposed* to) sexually, and every *other* way too, and every woman gets in super-good shape and learns how to actively control her sex life instead of passively waiting for the excitement to begin? Can you just imagine how many smiling, happy faces there'll be, because it's awfully hard (if not impossible) to be grumpy or mean or nasty when you've pleasured, and been pleasured by, someone you care enough about to trust your body with—and to share your love with.

One can only experience the ultimate "high" in love when one can surrender to another—the giving of one's self to someone in total trust. Some people argue about the word "surrender"—it frightens them because I don't think they understand it. When you surrender in love, you don't lose anything in yourself, you *gain* a feeling of the power of love—and of your self.

There are lots of ways to pleasure yourself. One of my favorites is filling a tub with warm water and bath oil or salts and then lying there sniffing the sensual fragrance and just thinking about all the good things in life you want—it's so lazy and relaxing. Another pleasurement is rubbing your whole body from face to toe with cream, letting it soak in, and then wrapping yourself in a terrycloth robe, turning on your favorite music and curling up with a new book and a bowl of oatmeal, honey and sunflower seeds with some milk floating along the top. Talk about sensuality—I think that one hits all the senses. Then there's massage. For the same money as a one-way cab fare to Kennedy Airport from midtown Manhattan, or the price of a Broadway theater ticket, you can have a masseur or a masseuse come to your pad and for one hour you can absolutely pass out from the pleasure of having almost every inch of your beautiful bod massaged. It's one of the great sensations of life. Now if you don't want to pay someone, ask your husby, wife, roomie or good friend if he or she will try it. Get some body lotion or oil and open your dining table out full, put a beach towel on it and go. Of course the only drawback when you don't pay is that usually you'll have to reciprocate (which actually works out pretty well —it's *great* exercise for your fingers, hands and arms, and it can also be a great turn-on!).

Dr. Wardell B. Pomeroy, a noted researcher and therapist, was quoted in *McCall's* about the ultimate self-pleasuring. Whether you agree or not about self-gratification, it's an interesting theory fostered by many doctors, psychiatrists, psychologists, ministers and teachers.

> Previously, myths about masturbation held it to be immature and harmful to health. These days masturbation is said to be more satisfying than intercourse. Masters and Johnson did find that, based on objective measurements of physiologic—not emotional—response, masturbation brings a more intense reaction than intercourse. Even though orgasm might be more easily brought about this way, the relationship between two people having sexual contact is preferred to solitary masturbation.

While we're on the subject, I'd like to repeat Woody Allen's classic lines from his movie *Love and Death*. He and a woman are resting atop a goose-down quilt, and she coos in his ear, "You're the greatest lover I've ever had," and Woody turns to her wide-eyed and says, "I practice a lot when I'm alone."

If you're lucky enough to have found the love of your life, that's terrific—but if not, don't deny yourself pleasure. Certainly love is the greatest pleasure in the world, but love has many faces and forms. I believe in feeling good so long as you don't hurt yourself or anyone else. The only thing that can hurt you is guilt, and if you love life and love, there's nothing to be guilty about. Pleasure yourself as often as you can—eat good food, breathe fresh air, use all your muscles, take care of your skin and your body—do all the things that make you feel better physically, mentally and emotionally.

Once you get your physical self in great shape, and your mental self sharpens up (which it will when your body is activated), and your emotional self softens and expands as the love increases in your life, you'll find the life forces growing greatly in every part of your physical, mental and emotional self. The ultimate expression of this life force is sex —a juicy, delicious, loving and exciting sex life. This is only *one* of the ways of pleasuring your self, but it is the ultimate.

The great turn-on for sex is love, and that's what this book is all about . . . love. When you have love oozing out of every pore, and love surrounding every thought, and love filling every feeling, then you'll know what life is *supposed* to be.

So work at getting healthy and I promise you you'll feel better than you've ever felt, you'll be happier than you've ever been, and you'll be pleasuring your self every day and loving every minute of it.

CHAPTER **2**

Pleasuring Me
Mentally

IF I CAN pleasure my body and put all
kinds of good things into it and use it beautifully
and keep it from getting fat and blubbery—why
can't I do the same thing for my mind?

Certainly physical pleasure is fantastic, but without the mental serenity to back it up, it doesn't reach
its full potential (and I want *all* the pleasure that's
possible). If I want every aspect of my life to be fun,
then the physical, mental and emotional pleasurings
all have to be fulfilled. You really can't ever separate
any part of your physical, mental or emotional lives
—they're all intertwined and always work (or don't
work) together.

If I can deliberately, through my own will, keep
all junk (coffee, booze, cigs, sugar, etc.) out of my

body, I can keep all junk (negative thoughts and fear) out of my mind. If I concentrate on putting only healthful things into my body like vites, Dynamite Milkshake and fresh foods, then I can concentrate on putting only positive thoughts and constructive ideas into my mind. It's just a matter of saying "I'll do it," and then following through and *doing* it. Disciplining my body is difficult (not eating ice cream or chocolate bars), but not impossible. Disciplining my mind is difficult too (refusing to repeat destructive gossip or to say any kind of downer about your self or anyone else), but certainly not impossible either.

And of course, when I begin to do this, any nonproductive or negative relationship in my life will fade away. If I'm feeling great physically and thinking great mentally, what in the world would I want with a destructive relationship emotionally? That's for a masochist who's probably not too well in any area, because to be well is to care for your self and to care for your self is to want only good things, which lead you to other good things. I happen to be a very analytical person—I analyze everything. "Why does that work that way?" "What did he mean when he said that?" "How can I improve my life?" The last one I've been analyzing since I was a little kid because I was in bad shape (no, *awful* shape) physically, mentally and emotionally, and I was very aware of my shortcomings and my needs to improve, so I was constantly trying to figure out how to change the things I hated about my self— and that was just about everything. Now Rome wasn't built in a day and neither was I. It's taken years and years, but I can honestly say that I'm a much better person now than I ever was (and I've still got a ways to go and I'm still working on it), and I'm just beginning to like my self. I remember many years ago I had a flash of an insight. I thought the bottom line, the real, basic essential of life, was to like yourself, because if you did, nothing around you could bother you. If you really believe you're a dynamite person, you'll act with confidence and become a doer and when you fail at something you'll go on trying till you achieve it. And if people try to drag you down and tell you you're not okay, you'll smile and walk away knowing you *are* okay, and don't need *them* to verify it or deny it. I said I had the flash of that insight, but I sure knew *I* didn't like myself at that point. I think I sort of did when I was a very little kid—not a lot, but I can remember liking some things about myself, but when I hit puberty, forget it; I became a self-loather. I almost despised myself, and I screwed up everything I tried to do. I'll never forget I was the champion speller through eight years of grade school—I won every prize without exception, and then at thirteen I went to high school and they had a giant spelling contest for the whole city and I became so nervous and tense that even though I beat every student in the preliminaries, when the main event came around I blew it with a simple word and a fella I had beat easily before won the grand prize. I was so tense I couldn't think straight, and I remember pacing up and down during the contest—I literally couldn't sit or stand still.

Now part of the change was in becoming a

woman—physically, mentally and emotionally it was difficult for me to adjust, but beyond that, every negative thought that was possible for me to think, I dwelt on. I *knew* I would lose the spelling contest, and in relationships it was the same. There was a very good-looking and popular guy at the all-boys school near my all-girls school, and though all my friends kept telling me he had eyes for me, I *knew* they were crazy and he'd never ask me out and he never did. He could probably sense my negativism and bad vibes, and I'm positive I acted in a way (because of my negative thinking) that repelled him. Later on, when I finally started to become aware of my negativism, it was a Herculean job to try to change myself, but I knew if I didn't, I'd never have *any* thing I wanted—that I'd screw up everything like I had in the past. So I deliberately tried to control my thoughts and keep the negs out, but, that is really hard! Slowly, though, it began to work—at least I was now *aware* of how negative I was. And it was almost like a religious thing: "If I expect bad to happen, then I won't be disappointed when it really does"—how does that grab you? Talk about expecting the worst to happen—I *knew* it would happen. I only got things I really didn't care about —the important things I definitely screwed up. Of course, I didn't know I was screwing them up then. I just figured I was unlucky and didn't really deserve to win. Then I stumbled on the Seven-Day Mental Diet from Emmet Fox's *Power Through Constructive Thinking,* and that was a turning point— thinking positively became a little easier until I gradually worked it into a habit that is now so strong that I won't allow any negative thought in my head. It became an obsession with me because I was by now very aware of how destructive negativism could be. So today I get kidded and it doesn't bother me at all. I just keep rolling along with my little positive thoughts working for me.

I'll never forget about a month after I opened in *Be Kind to People Week* Off-Broadway, I met a very attractive man who loved the show and me and the next day, in my dressing room, I got a huge bouquet of yellow roses with a card, which I saved. It had a stork on it, and printed above the stork was: CONGRATULATIONS ON YOUR NEW ARRIVAL, and under that he printed:

> *ME!*
> (How's that for positive!)
> Positively see you after the show!
> Love, Gemini

Then, the next day, I got another bouquet of yellow roses, with another card (he sent so many yellow roses there was hardly room for me!):

> Dear N.—May you always be positive
> in everything you do.
> Love, T.

I still have both cards pinned to my bookshelf. T. (who was also Gemini, and although one of the twins was adorable, the other wasn't) turned out to be one of the most negative persons I've ever met (I guess my positiveness didn't rub off), so our romance didn't quite last—thank God. I've been around enough negative people and it's exhausting watching them destroy themselves and constantly turning everything they say and do into the affirmative.

Karen DeCrow, past president of the National Organization for Women from 1974 to 1977, and an attorney and author, wrote a fabulous editorial in the New York *Times* not long ago, about how she pleasures herself. She called it "Forty, Single Again, and Absolutely No Regrets." She said that when she was a teenager, all she wanted was to "hook a guy," because that was the thing for a woman to do when she started college. Then, in her early twenties, when she was first married, someone told her to wear more makeup because her husband was working around good-looking secretaries and she wouldn't want to lose out to one of them. But now, she's just turned forty, and with two marriages behind her she finally feels in control of her life. She didn't put down marriage in her editorial, she just implied that her own two marriages didn't work. She says she's no longer skinny from the starvation diets without which one could never fit into a Merry Widow, but she's happy. And about herself and all women she says:

> We can be tough, we can be sexy, we can be smart, we can be tender. We are the new model Miss America. My life. I think I'll keep her.

Now here's a woman who's learning how to pleasure herself. She's not doing it at the expense of anyone else. She's finally learning how to make herself happy.

Having life fun and exciting and doing things we like to do are the beginnings of pleasuring ourselves. Once your body's in shape and feeling great, your enthusiasm for life will start taking over and mentally you will begin pleasuring your self in many different ways. The first thing is to find exactly what you want to do with your life. It's incredible how few people really know what they want out of life. Most people seem embarrassed to mention the fact that they want specific terrific things. But mostly people are earning a living doing things that either bore them or actively make them unhappy, and this is because they're not following their own personal aptitudes. Everyone has certain personality traits and mental and emotional inclinations that make them perfect for one line of work and absolutely wrong for another. So why not take an aptitude test and find out where you belong? I mentioned this in my "Energy" book, and received thousands of letters from people who said they did take an aptitude test and found out why they were so unhappy in their lines of work, and they wrote me how they were now looking around (while staying with their present jobs) for something the test showed would make them happy. One woman, however, wrote that she quit her job right after taking the test (which took a lot of guts), because she said she couldn't stand another day of it, and within a week she found a job she loved. She had been a typist in a big insurance office, and she found a job in a large department store in the cosmetic section where she now happily helps women decide on makeup colors and how to apply eye shadow, etc. Her test showed she was good with colors and with people, neither of which she could use in a large office, typing away. Another letter came in from a man with the opposite problem. He was a tire salesman for a major tire company, and hated it. His aptitude test showed that he wasn't good with people, but was terrific with ideas and figures, so he enrolled in a technology school while continuing to sell tires. He loves the classes and plans on quitting the selling job as soon as he gets his degree in computer programming. Both the woman and the man would have continued doing work they hated had they not taken the aptitude test and found they were going in the wrong directions.

I think every school (grammar and high) should have aptitude tests for kids to take. I mean, isn't finding out where your real interests lie much more important to your whole life than learning algebra, geometry or geography? You can be a whiz in math and know where every state capital is located, and wind up selling shoes when you should be the head pastry chef at the Waldorf-Astoria. If you're into flowers, but spend forty hours a week pouring concrete, you can't be too thrilled about it. And if your husband's driving a bus, and he's not keen on people, your home life won't be too groovy till he finds out the hard physical work of construction turns him on (and he doesn't have to talk to hundreds of people every day), or if your wife is sweating away eight hours at Bloomingdale's Junior Department when she'd really be happier turning out ad copy at

J. Walter Thompson, your home life will do a 90-degree turn when she starts working with words.

How many of us are lucky enough to have known from childhood exactly what we wanted to do? I know I didn't, and it took me years of doing dumb things I didn't like, to sort out what I did want to do. But what a waste of time. If someone had only told me about aptitude tests, I could have had extra years of happiness instead of frustration. But it's never too late to find out. And, fortunately, most libraries either have aptitude tests or can tell you where to go to take one.

Finding out where you belong is a mental pleasuring, and aside from finding your career, there are other mental pleasures it will bring you. Joanne Woodward, one of America's finest actresses, has decided she wants to study ballet, so she's begun ballet lessons, and the mental pleasure becomes physical pleasure as well when she does her exercises, which she loves.

Johnny Carson is a master magician, which pleasures him enormously. He is possibly the funniest person in the world. I once laughed at him so hard and so much at a benefit dinner for Ed Sullivan, that the pains in my stomach were excruciating. Everyone was praising Ed for helping talent to get ahead, and when Johnny's turn came, he told of all the great guests who *should* have been successes on Ed's show and become world famous, but that we never heard of: the trainer of the dancing bear who was hugged to death minutes before the show ("You never heard of *him*, did you?"); the man with incredible X-ray vision who could read a small sign two miles away, who was waiting off-camera to go on when Ed turned and said, "And here he is . . ." and stuck his pointed finger in the man's eye, and the man's never worked since ("You never heard of *him*, did you?"). Johnny went on with other losers, and the audience was literally hysterical—particularly me. Being funny is Johnny's job and he really works at it in preparation, but the magician thing is his fun, and he not only gives himself pleasure, but pleasures everyone around him.

Author Henry Miller, who's written over sixty books including *Tropic of Cancer*, has always believed in pleasuring himself and says he's lived a particularly happy life. When asked to write his epitaph, he said, "I'm going to beat those bastards." He says he was determined to survive and do what he wanted and he's pretty well done it. He says if he's not a rich man, at least he's a man who has pleased himself.

Warren Beatty is a romantic and one of his greatest pleasures is what he calls a "romantic science," astronomy. He spends lots of his relaxing time watching the stars and planets through his telescope. He says that the idea that long ago the people of early history saw the constellations as pictures in the evening sky is totally poetic, that it's imagination and technology at their best. He finds it mentally stimulating to look at the universe and watch for shooting stars. Warren is known as a great lover and I guess astronomy is his secondary pleasure because he does love women and they sure do love him back.

I met Bob Guccione, the founder and publisher of

Penthouse, when we were both guests on *AM-New York,* a terrific TV show in New York City, and was really impressed with his intellect and his gentleness (his good looks are an added extra). One tends to categorize, and I half expected a way-out macho kind of guy, and was very much surprised at how different Bob is. I asked him how he pleasures himself (ho-ho!) and he said, "Drawing. I get my biggest kicks with a pencil and pad." He used to be an expressionist painter—people and scenes—and he says, "The biggest driving force within me is the creative impetus—specifically painting. I get more pleasure from that than from almost anything else."

For the man known as "Mr. Credibility," Walter Cronkite away from the TV cameras is a great sailor. Just one of the things that over the years has given Walter a strong belief in himself is mastering the art of sailing. He also is a champion Charleston dancer, which amazes lots of people. To see him dance is an experience you won't soon forget. That this tall, handsome, distinguished newsman, who probably could have been elected president had he chosen to run (a national poll reported he would have won), dances like a pro is terrific. And watching him boogie at the top discos is fun because you don't expect him to be so hip.

John Travolta, who is one of the best and most sensitive actors around, has always loved airplanes. As a little kid he played with model planes—he built them, he flew them, he worked with them, he fixed them; they were his biggest passion. He always dreamed of being a flyer, he never gave up that belief that he would some day do it, and recently that belief and determination paid off. He got his pilot's license and is now able to fly to any place his heart desires. That same belief and determination led him to the lead in *Saturday Night Fever* which was one terrific performance, one of the best I've ever seen.

Is there something you've always wanted to do, like play the guitar, or learn French? You might be amazed to find that most colleges and some high schools and Y's have night courses where you can learn guitar-playing and French and public speaking and about a thousand other things.

Just the other day Marymount Manhattan College sent me their fall bulletin and just for fun I'd like to list a few of their courses:

Art of Making Artificial Silk Flowers
Assertiveness Training
Home Decorating Workshop
Painting
Personal Finance
Photo-Journalism
Baking Made Easy
Creative Job Hunting
How To Start Your Own Business
Techniques of Selling
Dance Exercise Workshop
Introduction to Wine
Treasures of Indian Art
Yoga
A Look at Sexuality
Law for the Consumer
Comedy Workshop

De-stressing Anger
Musical Theater Technique
Speedreading
Personal Decision-Making
Religion and Psychotherapy
Graphoanalysis: Handwriting Analysis

And these are only about one-quarter of the courses offered. The other seventy-five percent are just as interesting. No matter what it is you have always wanted to learn, or do, or be, there are courses at some school or Y in your area that can help you fulfill your dreams. All you have to do is ask around and maybe make a couple of phone calls to find out which places offer which subjects.

Can you imagine how you'll feel if you've always had a passion for old China and you enroll in a course on "The Treasure of Ancient China"? Or how self-reliant you'll feel after completing "End-of-Year Tax Strategies"? Or how exciting it will be starting your first novel after you finish the "Adventures in Writing" course? Maybe you'll wind up more successful than Jackie Susann or Norman Mailer.

And there's a course in the Marymount catalog called "The Psychology of Making Money" which sounds terrific from the description:

Learn how to become a money-maker by dealing with emotional conflicts, attitudes and values which interfere with financial progress and replacing them with successful money-making behavior. Discussion, sensitivity techniques and dream analysis will be among the methods employed to help students reach their financial goals.

Besides helping you to make money, some of this advice is sure to spill over into other areas of your life and help you become a happier person (and it *is* easier to be happy with money than without).

The New School in New York even has some technology-type courses like "Home Mechanics," which teaches home repair and improvement, and also workshops on carpentry and cabinet-making and even one on auto mechanics. The adult schools will teach you just about anything you've ever wanted to learn.

Now sometimes we have to go through pain to find pleasure, and if pain forces us to change our directions or our lives so they will lead to pleasure, then pain is good. Suzanne Gordon wrote in a recent New York *Times* article that pain is very important and useful and necessary in teaching us to avoid physical and emotional damage. Just as we will pull our hand immediately out of a fire when we feel the pain through the nerves in our hand, emotional pain is also a call for action. We need anxiety because it's a signal for us to prepare to deal with problems. She tells us that Freud describes some of the most traumatic problems that are the hardest to overcome as those where an attack takes place so quickly that there's no time for anxiety, and because of this, mastery is almost impossible.

Then she says that many psychologists tell us to deny that pain exists, that they believe that divorce can magically become "creative," that you can finish your love affair or marriage and go on to the next one like you finish breakfast and go on to lunch. They tell you to get rid of all pain and trauma and not to delve into the whys that could possibly teach us what went wrong and keep us from entering another bad relationship. The psychologists tell us to get rid of the painful feelings but not the situations that cause the pain, and go about doing our thing. They tell us not to flee but to stay.

She says that if we follow their advice we lose the only reason for pain, which is not endurance of it, but a strong impulse to really change what needs to be changed.

Sometimes we can learn from the pain felt in the psychiatrist's office. Both Doris Day and her son, Terry Melcher, have been helped through therapy. After Doris' second husband, Marty Melcher, died, and she found that she was bankrupt because of some of her late husband's business dealings, she hit the pits and started going to a psychiatrist. Then Terry was almost killed in a motorcycle accident, and the two of them feel that through therapy they've gotten to a point where their own relationship was improved, as well as their outlook on the many problems they've both encountered.

Woody Allen says he always wanted to be another person and, through therapy, he's seeking to find out why, so he can start being himself and enjoying it. And Julie Andrews went to a psychiatrist because the public sees her as a Goody-Two-Shoes while *she* sees herself as a sex symbol and the frustration is overwhelming. Al Pacino had the reverse problem. He was bothered by all his women fans wanting him, but he says they're only interested in Pacino, the symbol, not Pacino, the real person. He says that that kind of adulation is alienating and can drive you crazy.

Ali MacGraw has been in therapy for a while and feels her whole life has changed for the better. After the painful divorce with Bob Evans and the subsequent loss of the lead female role in *The Great Gatsby* because of the divorce (Evans was the producer and didn't feel he could cope with seeing Ali's face every day in the rushes, so even though making the flick was her idea, Mia Farrow got the coveted part of Daisy), and the newer painful split from Steve McQueen, she says she's happier now than she's ever been. She's now totally on her own for the first time ever and she loves it. She's had her passport, driver's license and all other legal documents changed to her own name. She says Ali MacGraw is who she is in reality and legally and she's glad she's finally there.

John Lennon, Liv Ullman, Marlon Brando, Tuesday Weld, Kris Kristofferson, Dyan Cannon, John Denver, Peter Sellers and Raquel Welch all are going or have gone into therapy, and they all believe it's been helpful in their lives.

All of these things take discipline (not to eat sugar and junk, to jog every day, wash your face before going to bed), but I've found that imagination is much stronger than will when it comes to asking myself to do things. When I force myself to do something I don't feel like doing at the moment, I will do it, but resentfully. I am extremely self-disciplined (after years of struggle) and can literally make myself do anything, but I've found a better way. Like sometimes, when I'm running late for a morning appointment and I really don't want to do my morning exercises, well, I used to make myself do them anyway, but there was a little tension and I did them faster than usual because I really didn't want to do them at that time, and that tension made them harder to do. So I figured out how to create a desire in my mind so that I would really want to do them always. I visualize myself feeling absolutely and incredibly great and full of power in every part of my body, and I image-in to my mind that each exercise is truly going to make every last part of me feel sensational. The beauty part is, this does create a desire to do them, and in the long run, the exercises *will* change your mind and your body for the better. It may take time, but it definitely will happen.

Before I got into yeast and lecithin and vites, while I was drinking coffee and smoking, every part of my body was full of tension, particularly my eyes. I'd wake up in the morning and my eyes would be so dry I could hardly blink. I went to several doctors and they couldn't find the cause and I asked if it could be from tension (some people get hit in the stomach, some get pimples, etc.) and they said yes and wanted to give me tranquilizers. Now I'd been there before and drugs scare me and turn me off, and I sure didn't want to start again. So I figured out how to overcome "dry eyes" myself. I noticed that any time I gagged on anything in my throat, it made my eyes water, so I stuck my finger down my throat and gagged and sure enough, it made tears. So I hooked "gagging" onto the front end of my "chewing exercise," which a throat specialist had given me for my tense throat (can you believe all my old tension?), and I've kept it up every morning at the end of my sit-ups and before my mental and emotional exercises. I gag myself three times, then I chew very broadly about 100 times and *voilà!* My eyes are relaxed and so is my throat.

I don't know if you're aware of how much energy your eyes use up, but I was amazed when I found out it's a very large percentage of your total body energy. When you think about it, it makes sense. When you're awake your eyes are constantly in action. Wherever you go, whatever you do, you're using your eyes—walking down the street, window-shopping, people-watching, going to a flick, just sitting quietly, your eyes are being used. And when your body's tense from coffee, cigarettes or too much reading, your eyes get tense and you expend even *more* energy.

Besides my "dry eyes" exercise, I learned a terrific exercise to relax eye-tension. I do it whenever I feel my eyes getting strained. Not too long ago I did a TV show in Boston and the co-host was Bob Cummings, who is a really vital man. Anyway, he showed me his "Elephant Swing," which is easy to do and really relaxes all the tension in your eyes. You stand up with your feet about a foot or a foot and a half apart, let your arms hang loosely by your sides, and then slowly start swinging your head, torso and arms from side to side, keeping your feet in place. As your head swings loosely around, keep your eyes open and deliberately don't focus on anything, so that as your eyes are swept from side to side you will see only a blur, as if you were riding in a train and didn't focus on anything so that the countryside would whiz past and you'd just be aware of the blur. Count out loud as you swing back and forth and do this sixty times, being sure to relax your eyes and not focus on anything—just keep it a blur, as your head, arms and shoulders turn. Not only does the tension leave your eyes, it leaves your whole head and you'll feel a super relaxation taking over.

It's not only important to do exercises, but it's important to do specific ones. And it's up to each person to create his or her own. Most of the ones I do started out plain and simple and through my imagination I've changed each one to fit me and my special needs. For instance, in my "Energy" book I told about the yoga deep-breathing exercise I do in bed first thing every morning when I wake up. Well, since then I've changed it a little and it really works better for me now. Originally, I relaxed my body lying on my back in bed, slowly exhaled every inch of stale air through my mouth, held it for a count of ten, then inhaled very slowly through my nose till my lungs were completely filled—held it for a count of fifty, then very slowly exhaled through my mouth, and repeated this four more times. Now I do exactly that the first time and then, when I've got the second inhalation, instead of holding it, I use my diaphragm muscles (the muscles at the base of my lungs) to pant (through my nose) fifty times, then exhale slowly through my mouth. The third time I do it the old way (holding my breath for a count of fifty), then the fourth time I pant fifty times again through my nose using my diaphragm muscles (it feels like your stomach muscles), and keeping the rest of my body perfectly relaxed, then slowly exhale, and the fifth time do it the original way. The panting strengthens all the muscles in the diaphragm so they get used to breathing deeper all the time. I noticed that if I panted much more than fifty times, my shoulders would start to feel a twinge, so the diaphragm must be connected to the shoulders somehow, and the shoulders are usually the first place tension sets in when you're under stress so this new part of the exercise is working different parts of my body, which need it, and relaxing them, and all the additional oxygen that this puts in my lungs helps my brain to think more clearly, and this pleasures me a lot mentally.

As you're doing your exercises try to think of little ways you can make each exercise unique to *you*. You may be amazed at how different things will pop into your mind about ways to improve them for your self. And it'll make each exercise a personal part of you.

Another kind of exercise that can contribute to pleasuring your self mentally is self-hypnosis. I've used this technique successfully to lose weight. Usually I'm able to keep my weight down where I want it because I'm really healthy, and a healthy person can't be too fat or too thin, but whenever I take a birth control pill (hereafter called "the pill"), I find it puts on anywhere from five to ten pounds. This is because of the hormonal changes the pill makes in your body, and I've been advised that a woman should take it for nine months and lay off it for three months, and then start the cycle over, because the pill simulates pregnancy, which only lasts nine months, so taking the pill longer than that can have a negative effect. Of course every woman should check with her own gynecologist about this.

Anyway, whenever I do take the pill, I gain a few pounds and they're usually impossible to lose. Then I discovered how self-hypnosis can do the trick. Not just plain old general self-hypnosis ("I'm losing weight" or "I'm getting thin")—that didn't work for me. I sat down and tried to figure out how I could get my subconscious to work for me in dropping those few pounds, and my Giant Self led me to this: the reason I am overweight is because the pill puts hormones in my body that seem to stimulate my appetite and hold water in my cells—so if I use self-hypnosis, I should not be general ("I am losing weight") but specific ("I am losing my appetite). And I tried it. And it works. I said to myself, "I am losing my appetite, I am not hungry, my stomach feels satisfied, I am losing my appetite." And suddenly I stopped feeling hungry! That sometimes compulsive desire for food dwindled and disappeared. But I didn't do this just once in a while. I did it many times through the day. I started mid-morning looking in a mirror into my eyes and kept repeating, "I am not hungry, I'm losing my appetite," and my subconscious took over and eliminated my desire for food.

Try it. It's truly amazing what the subconscious will do for you through self-hypnosis if you'll only use it. I lost five pounds and keep it off by daily repeating to myself that I'm not hungry. Sometimes I even say it to myself while I'm eating, and I eat less than I usually would—it's painless because when your appetite goes away, you really don't want much food and you find you feel good with a lot less.

Mental pleasure depends a lot on your self-image and anything you can do to improve your self is important. Up till fairly recently I used to do my own nails. Well, sort of. My nails were usually not too gorgeous because I picked at them. Not the nails, but the skin around them. I used to pick till they bled. I know it sounds awful and it was. I guess it was a kind of masochism because the more it hurt the more I did it, and I did it most of my life. I tried to stop a million times, but it never worked. Finally, a few months ago, I looked at how awful they looked and decided then and there to finally give it a last try. I looked in the Yellow Pages under nail care, found a place a block away on Lexington Avenue, called and made an appointment. The woman looked at the mess and suggested a new kind of false nail that's permanent (it grows out with your own nail and must be redone every six or eight weeks; after several months your nails are long and stronger and then you have the long tips wrapped with paper and keep it up forever). So I (being desperate) said okay. Well, my nails were so beautiful when she got through (and like steel, they were so strong), that to this day I haven't picked at them even one time. It made me think of a true story I heard a few years ago of an experiment done at a prison. They took average, "nice," un-sadistic people and put them in charge of the inmates, and eventually the "nice" guards started becoming mean and sadistic. The explanation was that when people are servile or demeaned or in a lowly, cowering position, it tends to bring out the worst in their overlings. The experimenters concluded that it's human nature to treat a coward or a fearful person badly— that courage commands respect and fear commands disrespect. In the case of my nails, as long as they looked awful I made them look even worse. But now that they're looking good I keep them looking good. I used to hate my hands for looking so awful, but now I respect them and it's a terrific feeling. So the better you make yourself look, the better you'll like your self and the better you'll treat your self. Amen.

So when you're pleasuring your self, remember that you're not the only one benefitting from it— that when you make your self happy and feel good, it's contagious and will make everyone around you feel terrific too!

Faith-full To Me

HAVE YOU BEEN cheating on your self? I know it sounds ridiculous, but lots of us cheat on our selves every day. For example, did you skip your Dynamite Milkshake and vites (it only takes two minutes) and make an excuse for not doing your morning exercise (only ten minutes), and take a cab or your car instead of walking the few blocks to work, and have the martinis for lunch even though you know they make you sleepy all afternoon, and the double chocolate mousse for dessert when you've been trying so hard to drop a few pounds? Or did you let your husband think you really enjoyed last night's lovemaking when, if you'd just explain to him that a tiny bit of romance really turns you on, you could really groove with him? Or did you let your wife think you like lima beans with caraway seeds when lima beans with garlic would ecstasize you?

Faith-full to me means having lots of faith in myself—really believing in my own possibilities. To believe in yourself, you must be true to your self. And you don't even have to be terribly motivated. If you just do *some* of the things I suggest—just take action and *do* them, even if you don't totally understand why—you will begin to have a stronger belief in your self. For instance, if I tell you that it's of the utmost importance to have a healthy body before you can hope to do anything with your life and you think I'm probably right but you're not positive but you start to take the shake and vites and begin to do some simple exercises anyway, just the mental discipline to get yourself started is a big step.

Mental discipline is probably the most crucial factor needed to change the direction of one's life. I know my mental discipline is incredible because I've trained it. I can make myself do *anything*—I am in charge of my mind, and once I get it set for something I want, nothing can stop me. I wasn't always this way, but lots of work got me disciplined and it's a great feeling knowing you're in charge of your self—that you can literally make yourself do anything you want.

So just getting yourself started on an improvement plan via the shake and vites is an important step, because once you start feeling better physically, you'll start thinking more clearly and it'll become easier to eliminate the negative things holding you back in life. Where it used to be fuzzy thinking, and the negatives weren't so easy to recognize, once your head clears up you'll see them easily and kick them out. And the knowledge that you told yourself to do something (taking the shake and vites) and you followed through, will boost your self-esteem and self-reliance (you can really rely on yourself).

Let me show you how becoming healthy and using mental discipline created a belief in me that not only didn't exist before, but was so far out of my reach that I didn't think it could *ever* exist. Until fairly recently I didn't sing. I didn't sing because I *couldn't* sing. I'd always wanted to sing but I couldn't. I can remember when I was in the second grade and our class used to line up in the hall with all the other classes and we would salute the flag and then sing "The Star-Spangled Banner." I was so tense that the poor notes trying to get past my tight throat came out strangled. It used to embarrass me because the other kids would turn around when I sang and stare at me because I sounded so awful. It was sad because I wanted to sing more than anything else in the world, and I vowed that some day I would learn. Time went on and I seemed to get worse (I didn't know it but I was getting tenser). When I was a teenager, my boyfriend used to have a contest to see who sang worse, me or him. The thing that was so humiliating was that he didn't care about singing, he didn't want to sing and didn't care if he had a terrible voice, whereas I desperately wanted to sound good and didn't. One time he brought a little cassette and recorded both of us singing solo (I didn't believe I sounded worse than he did), and I heard myself for the first time and was devastated—(I did).

So I started working on my off-hours with a piano player, but I never got better. But I also never gave up. I worked with quite a few piano players (needless to say, I had to pay them) and maybe I improved a *little*, but not noticeably. The tension in my throat was incredible. I had tension all through my body, but it seemed to come out in my throat the most (some people get ulcers because the tension centers in their stomach—we all have different weaknesses).

Then, as I told you in the first chapter, I conked out physically, went to the hospital, and through reading Adelle Davis found out about vitamins and tension and invented my Dynamite Milkshake, which totally turned my life around. The tension started to leave, and I couldn't believe it but my voice started to sound better. As I got more relaxed, the tension in my throat relaxed and my voice started to sound un-strangled. (When I was a little kid my mother had to break an aspirin in quarters and wrap each piece in bread to get it down my throat—that's how constricted my poor throat was.)

Well, now, my body's so super-relaxed and all that previously trapped energy's released, I starred in an Off-Broadway musical, *Be Kind to People Week*, singing my little heart out, and I sang the title song in a movie we're completing now, *The Perils of P.K.*, and I recorded two albums. I sent one album to my old flame with the terrible voice, who still can't believe it's me singing—he says I must have paid someone else to do it, it *can't* be me!

If I can do it, so can you. And I'm sure there aren't too many who would need to go from one extreme to another like I did.

To be faith-full to yourself, you must follow through when you really want something. Art Linkletter says, "You haven't really failed as long as you don't quit. You may have missed. You may have struck out, but the game isn't over." Art told me the story of how he got started in broadcasting. He was very young and waiting backstage to go on as an emcee, and he was so paralyzed with fright that he couldn't go on. Then he realized that if he didn't, he'd never be anything but a scared failure and that thought mobilized him to action and he went out and was a smash hit.

Michael Caine believes he owes his incredible success as an actor to a schoolteacher who told him he was never going to amount to anything, that he was born to be a "low-class worker." The shock of what the teacher said hit him because it was said as a cold fact, not out of anger or malice. It scared Michael and made him aware that if he didn't do something about it, that's exactly what would happen, so he took stock of himself and figured out that reading was the key to knowledge. Then he began to read fourteen books a week, which seems staggering until you realize how determined Michael was to become somebody. He says he read so much that his eyesight weakened, forcing him to wear glasses almost constantly. But his determination paid off, and in looking back he feels that he was fortunate that his teacher shocked him into action.

When you believe in yourself, you don't worry about things that have already happened or about things that might happen. The most famous insurance company on earth, Lloyd's of London, has made millions out of the inclination of people to worry about things that seldom happen. Lloyd's of London bets people that whatever they are worrying about will never happen, but they don't call it betting, they call it insurance. That covers worrying about the future. But what about worrying about the past? The late Fred Fuller Shedd, editor of the Philadelphia *Bulletin,* asked a college graduating class how many of them had ever sawed wood, and most of the students raised their hands. Then he asked how many of them had ever sawed sawdust and of course no one raised a hand. He pointed out how ridiculous it is to try to saw sawdust because it's already sawed, and it's the same with the past. When you begin to worry about things that are behind you, you are trying to saw sawdust. The only way to use our past mistakes is to analyze them and figure out how never to make the same mistake again.

Liv Ullman, in her marvelous autobiography, *Changing,* talks about the breakup of her long love affair with Ingmar Bergman, which produced a daughter, Linn. Liv says she used to dream about a great togetherness with Ingmar and she was sure that they could achieve it. But then, when the final split came, she knew they would never be together as a unit again, and when the breakup came she wept and felt like a deserted thirteen-year-old child instead of a thirty-year-old woman. She then realized that it was impossible to live her life as if it could only be fulfilled through another person, to seek refuge in someone else from what was *her* loneliness and insecurity. Ingmar was no longer a part of her personal life, and nothing could change that fact. But she still had her self, and contact with her own being, and she began to make better contact with others, who, she found, respected her more when she became independent and stopped cling-ing, stopped relying so desperately on others for her own happiness.

We all do this or have done it at some time in our lives, and why wouldn't we? Wasn't childhood fun for most of us, with few cares and mummy and pops footing the bills and making sure we had the three squares? Playing Peter Pan is fun for a while, but it leads to emotional disaster if we keep it up too long. Once we're beyond childhood, how can we expect someone else to assume total responsibility for us, to take care of us? Now I admit it's an easy trap to fall into, and I have lots of times, but it never can work out. First of all, we lose respect for our selves when we are not self-reliant, when we cling to and depend on someone else for everything. And when we don't respect our selves everyone can sense this (believe me, it's a cinch to spot a clinger, even an unobvious one), and immediately others lose their respect for us. We love people who rely on themselves, we are attracted to self-motivated, confident people who don't need us. Of course we all have moments of need, but I'm not talking about that. We all have our ups and downs when we need certain things like a loan of money, or somebody's ear to listen to a problem and help us solve it, or warmth and af-fection when we're in a down mood. We can be terribly self-reliant and still have a momentary need. And just knowing there are friends out there who'll run when we call is a terrific feeling.

Diane von Furstenberg is a beautiful, intelligent and successful woman. She has one of the most prestigious lines of designer clothes, perfume and cosmetics, and she's written a wonderful book, *Diane von Furstenberg's Book of Beauty.* I met Diane a couple of years ago when she did a TV commercial for the Citizen's Committee for New York City, Inc., with me and Otto Preminger and Skitch Henderson about how much we all love New York. Besides all her physical and mental attributes, Diane's a very loving person. She believes strongly in love and that a person's life should be shared with another person. She also believes that everything in life is aimed at being a great lover—of loving and being loved, and that we create things—from a new hairstyle to a successful business enterprise—so that we can feel we deserve love. She says that in her own self-discovery she's found she's done everything in life so that she could earn love, and that it's the things about yourself that you're not even aware of that are usually loved, like your vulnerability (that part of you that's afraid to be hurt). Diane says she can't live without love and warmth and without a person to love and care for and to do things for and to be beautiful for.

Diane also believes that the greatest natural enemy of women is insecurity, and to overcome this and to be a complete and happy woman you must be independent. She says that to be happy with a man, a woman must know that she could leave him and take care of herself (and of course that advice goes for men too). To stay with someone just because he supports you financially and pays all the bills, and because you don't feel that you could take care of yourself, is a major cause of insecurity. Diane believes that every woman should have an identity of her own that is separate from the man in her life, which can come either through a career or, if you have a strong sense of your self and are a complete person, you can find it in your home. The point is, if you have a choice and are secure in the knowledge that you are self-reliant, you will be a happy and productive person.

I read a great deal, and my favorite books are biographies and autobiographies. Before I started reading about other people's lives, I used to think that my problems were unique, that my emotional traumas were the most horrendous and that my mental quandaries were the most perplexing. But once I started delving into other people's lives, I learned that *all* people have emotional traumas and mental quandaries. Even the ones who seem like they don't, do. When, I read Lilli Palmer's terrific autobiography, *Change Lobsters and Dance,* I learned about her courage during the emotional crisis in her marriage to Rex Harrison (or I should say crises, because he gave her quite a few). Lilli was and is a beautiful woman and actress, and she suffered immensely during her marriage to Harrison. She had lots of happiness with him too, and that's what made it so traumatic—if we only suffer, it's not so difficult to break up a relationship. But the memories of the good times make it heart-wrenching. Well, Lilli pulled together all her inner forces and resources and weathered the storms, finally finding the courage to divorce Rex, and she found lasting happiness with another, much younger actor, Carlos Thompson. But the pain she lived through was enormous and I feel heartened after reading about a person conquering such problems and coming out happier than ever. It's heartening to read about a courageous person. We sense that the same courage is inside each of us, just waiting to be used.

Not long ago I finished another biography, volume two of *Jennie* (Lady Randolph Churchill, Winston Churchill's mother) by Ralph G. Martin. Jennie was born in 1854 and died in 1921, and did more with her life in those pre-feminist days than the majority of women are doing today. After her husband, Lord Randolph, died from syphillis (she stayed by his side until the end, and because of this, she lost her one great love, Count Kinsky, who wouldn't wait any longer for her and married another woman), she had a scandalous love affair with George Cornwallis-West. It was scandalous because George was only two weeks older than her son Winston, a major affront to public opinion in those days. But Jennie's favorite motto was, "They say? What *do* they say? *Let* them say!"

Besides having incredible sex appeal, Jennie was an astute businesswoman—extremely capable and inventive. She organized and managed a hospital ship, she founded and became editor and publisher of an impressive literary magazine, *The Anglo-Saxon Review,* she wrote a book, *Reminiscences,* and she wrote several plays, one of which had a fairly successful run. She said about herself, "I love people. I love the world. I love life." Reading about this incredible woman's life makes me feel terrific because I know she overcame unbelievable odds and resistance to her success, but she never gave up. She believed in her self and was faith-full to her self, and certainly believed in and lived a life of love.

Winston Churchill always gave his mother most of the credit for his success—she promoted him as a beginning writer and a beginning politician, and he said without her help that he never would have made it.

Winston, although he never went to college, became one of the most important men in the twentieth century. He made a statement many years ago and it's one of my all-time favorite quotations:

> Courage is the most important of all the qualities because it's the only one that assures all of the others.

Guts, chutzpah—that, with determination, will get you almost anything you want (in fact, I believe it will get you *anything!*). To me, guts implies a great belief in God (or Giant Self or Source or Spirit or Love) because guts implies there is fear that is overcome (if you're not afraid, then you don't need courage), and the inner strength comes from the knowledge that you're not alone, that something inside is protecting you and leading you on. What else can overcome fear? If you think about it, nothing else can. If you're scared to death of something, really petrified, you'll either freeze and do nothing, or some thought consciously or subconsciously will tell you that you're stronger than the fear, and you'll be mobilized into action. The conscious or subconscious thought is that there is something bigger than you which is taking over, and when it does take over, the fear disappears.

Loving your self is the most important thing in the world. Certainly we don't love our negative qualities, but we can love all the goodness inside ourselves. Some people have lots of goodness near the surface, and in some others the goodness is way down deep under the surface where it's hard to see and feel, but the point is, it *is* there someplace. When you finally become aware of how important it is to truly care for your self, that's when you'll become aware that you don't have to love *all* of your self—just finding one good quality is a terrific start. Now everybody has at least *one* good quality—be it a love of nature (even if you think you despise most people) or a love of color or a love of gadgets or a love of fixing things (like broken steering wheels or chipped dishes). Once you find something about yourself that's terrific (even if it's really teeny to start with), then you can begin to develop that quality. And the more it grows, not only will you like your self more, but you'll also start to find other seeds of goodness that can be watered. Eventually your positive qualities will outnumber your negative ones, and that's when you'll *really* start to dig your self (as will everyone else).

Dr. George Weinberg and I did a TV interview show together and became friends. He's written a wonderful book, *Self Creation,* which is about just that—creating a new self. One of his chapters is about how to be liked and in it he says:

The way to be liked—the right way—is to cultivate qualities that you can like in yourself. Qualities that seem so worthwhile to you that the people you really want for your friends ought to like you for them. Then work on developing these qualities for their own sake, for your own sake, without trying to impress anyone else. In a way, being liked always has to come second, like having an orgasm in sex or becoming famous as a writer or painter. If it's your main goal, you can ruin not only your chances for success but also your capacity for enjoyment.

Sometimes to build up our own confidence, we idealize our past and that's okay. I know I always try to build my self up to compensate for having thought I was a nothing for such a long time. Just recently my brother and I found some old report cards from grammar school and we got hysterical reading them. Both of us had fantasized ourselves as having been brilliant kids, and when we saw a few "C's," we couldn't believe it.

Miller Upton, ex-president of Beloit College, was quoted in *Sunshine* magazine, about being for the "upperdog":

> I have just about reached the end of my tolerance for the way our society now seems to have sympathetic concern only for the misfit, the pervert, the drug addict, the drifter, the chronic criminal, the underachiever. It seems to me we have lost touch with reality and become warped in our attachments. I feel it is time for someone like me to stand up and say, in short, "I'm for the upperdog!"
>
> I'm for the achiever—the one who sets out to do

something and does it; the one who recognizes the problems and opportunities at hand, and endeavors to deal with them; the one who is successful at his immediate task because he is not worrying about someone else's failings; the one who doesn't consider it "square" to be constantly looking for more to do, who isn't always rationalizing why he shouldn't be doing what he is doing; the one, in short, who carries the work of his part of the world squarely on his shoulders.

To create a decent society, our first task is to help each individual be decent unto himself and in his relationship with other individuals.

We will never create a good society, much less a great one, until individual excellence and achievement are not only respected but encouraged.

That is why I am for the upperdog—the achiever, the succeeder.

I agree with this a great deal because I am a hard worker, an achiever, but I'm also aware of all the help I had along the way. Had I not gotten sick and discovered vites and invented my milkshake, I would have continued being a tense, anxious, and depressed person who was getting in my own way. I never would have had the physical strength to cope with my mental and emotional problems. Even though I know it sounds terribly dramatic, it's nevertheless true that I positively don't believe I would be alive today, much less a super-energetic person trying to succeed. Because I was there, I can understand how awful it is to doubt yourself in every way and be afraid of failure and just about everything else. My Giant Self or Source led me to my sickness, which led me to the shake and vites, which led me to physical strength which I needed for mental and emotional strength. I know what it's like to take a drink to bolster your confidence because you're scared, I know what it's like to talk yourself out of doing something because you think everyone else is better or smarter or more talented or more capable. I know what it's like to be so depressed that you really don't want to go on living, you don't see any purpose in living under such a worthless existence. I believe that this kind of tension and anxiety and depression leads to crime and murder and suicide. So it's one thing to be for the upperdog, but it's just as important to understand the underdog—not to coddle or placate or baby, but to understand, and try to help. People need help— I need help and you need help. We all do. We all need physical energy to combat tension and depression. We all need pride in ourselves. We're *all* achievers—it's just that some of us haven't the confidence to realize what we have going for us and to bring it out and express it. I hit the pits—my tension and depression would have led me, not to rob or steal or murder someone else but to murder my self. I thought about it a lot (I don't think there can be any lower mental, emotional or physical state than to consider ending your own life), and because of this, I have tremendous empathy for others suffering like I used to. Those who know me today say they can't believe that a person with my enormous energy and zest for life could ever have been that low. I know it may seem hard to believe, but it's true. And the memory of it is so vivid in my mind that nothing, *nothing* could stop me from taking my shake and vites every day of my life. I've lugged my blender to almost every area of the world, plus the bottles and jars of vites and yeast and lecithin, and the goading force is the memory of what my life used to be like before I started on the shake and vites. I can only say it changed my life so totally and made me such a different person, that I want to tell everyone in the whole world about it. If I can save one person from the agonies I used to experience, it will mean a great deal to me. This is why I'm giving the Dynamite Milkshake to prisons and mental health institutes and not making any money on it. There but for the grace of God go I. My source is taking fantastic care of me, and when other people start taking the shake and vites, I know they'll discover their Source (or Giant Self) and the world is going to be a lot happier and more fun. And then everyone can appreciate his or her own abilities and start expressing them and become achievers, and the world will only be full of upperdogs. Just the thought of it turns me on. The worst thing that can happen is that people in institutes will start eating better breakfasts, and it'll be free. And the best thing would be maybe it *will* make a difference. And it's letting me express the incredible gratitude I feel for having crawled out of the pits and the knowledge that if *I* did, others can too, and once they get out, like me they won't ever have to fall back in again.

In Milton Mayeroff's book, *On Caring*, he tells about self-actualization through caring:

There is a selflessness in caring that is very different from the loss of self in panic or through certain kinds of conformity. It is like the selflessness that goes with being absorbed in something I find genuinely interesting, that goes with being "more myself." Such selflessness includes heightened awareness, greater responsiveness to both the other and myself, and the fuller use of my distinctive powers.

In caring for the other, in helping it grow, I actualize myself.

So by caring or loving another (a person or another part of you, your Giant Self or Source), you do become more yourself, and the more aware you become of your true self, the more courage you will have and then the more you'll believe in your self.

Mayeroff continues:

Besides trusting the other, I must also trust my own capacity to care. I must have confidence in my judgments and in my ability to learn from mistakes; I must, as we say, trust my instincts.

To care for another person, I must be able to understand him and his world as if I were inside it. But only because I understand and respond to my own needs to grow can I understand his striving to grow; I can understand in another only what I can understand in myself.

Then he says:

Just as I may be indifferent to myself, use myself as a thing, or be a stranger to myself, so I may care for myself by being responsive to my own needs to grow.

I become my own guardian, so to speak, and take responsibility for my life. . . .

No one else can give me the meaning of my life; it is something I alone can make. The meaning is not something predetermined which simply unfolds; I help both to create it and to discover it, and this is a continuing process, not a once-and-for-all.

Once you start to trust yourself, you'll be amazed at the things you'll find you intuitively know and feel. It happened to me. All my life I wanted to learn how to eat with chopsticks. Every time I went to a Chinese restaurant, I'd try . . . and try . . . and never did I pick up on it. I'd always ask the different Chinese waiters to show me how, and they would patiently put one chopstick in position in my hand, and then the other one, and they'd try to show me how to do it, but it never worked. I just didn't get the hang of it. I remember going to one restaurant on West Fifty-sixth Street in New York City and being very happy when the chopsticks came folded in a piece of paper, and on the paper were printed instructions on how to use them. Well, I spent about thirty minutes painstakingly going through every step of the instructions, and either one chopstick would fall out of my tentative grip or the food plopped back down on the plate. At one point I got so frustrated that I speared each morsel and ate everything that way—skewered on one chopstick. Oh, I was discouraged (but I would never give up!). So I kept trying new Chinese restaurants, hoping that someday some terrific Chinese waiter would finally clue me in to the secret of chopsticks. Then, one night about four years ago, for some unknown reason, I picked up the chopsticks and didn't try to figure out the exact positioning of each stick and how to hold one firm and wiggle the other (like I had been told)—I just picked them up and let my intuition or instinct or *something* guide me, and I literally couldn't believe it but the food was actually being picked up and got all the way to my mouth without falling. It was incredible to me. All those years I was focusing on the right way to use chopsticks and this night I just relaxed and let my subconscious guide me, and it worked. I didn't think about *how* I was doing it, I was just doing it, and it was so simple it was ridiculous. It just amazes me that all those years I was trying so hard and it's really so simple and easy.

The same with disco dancing (or creative dancing, we calls it!). Sure you can try to learn routines and steps, but it's all in the feeling. If you just move with the music you'll not only do it right, you'll feel it right. Sometimes we get in our own way, but that's generally when we're not in tune with our selves, when we don't trust ourselves and our intuition.

Jill Clayburgh is a beautiful woman and a fine actress. She lives in and loves New York, and although until recently she'd never been married, she'd lived with two men, Al Pacino for five years, and playwright David Rabe, whom she married not long ago. When Pacino split right after *The Godfather*, Jill suffered immensely and lived through pain, anger, fear and self-loathing, but she pulled herself together and not only did she make an emotional comeback, but her career really soared. She won the Cannes Film Festival Award for Best Actress for her performance in *An Unmarried Woman.* To Jill, emotional intimacy is important, but for whatever reasons, she'd been hesitant about getting married. However, with the same determination with which she came out of the bust-up with Pacino and climbed to stardom, she overcame this fear and feels she will succeed in her relationships.

Warren Beatty believes in himself and has worked hard to attain that belief. He says that although he does love himself (which is positive), he's not "in love with himself," because to do that you have to take yourself too seriously and he has too great a sense of humor for that to happen.

Geraldine Fitzgerald is a sensational person and a fine actress. She's a warm and witty (and fiery) Irish person, who knows what she wants and how to go about getting it. Geraldine is now in her sixties and she wears her hair long and loose, even though she says, "A woman's expected to put her hair up permanently after a certain age. She's definitely not supposed to let her hair fall free around her face." But Geraldine has always had the guts to live the way *she* wanted to, and not long ago she did her first nightclub act singing Irish songs of the streets, which was sensational, and cut her first record album. She says, "Life begins when you want it to!"

Monique van Vooren is not only Belgian and beautiful, she is also determined, and that determination has led her to a string of successes as an actress and a singer and is now driving her to write her first novel, *Night Sanctuary.* She recently wrote

The Happy Cooker, or recipes for two people (aphrodisiac dinners, drinks and dishes, she says). Monique started out with a not-too-strong ego (as did *all* the celebrities I've talked to), and the acting and singing boosted it, and now the writing, which is a really visible accomplishment, is strengthening her ego even more. *Nobody* can be successful if he or she accepts a weak ego and lets it stay weak—those who strive for accomplishment can actually feel their egos get healthier and stronger. And Monique is heading in the right direction. She says that every day she gets more self-reliant because every day she's proving to her self that she can ask her self to do things (like writing the novel) and her self is coming through.

Regine owns twelve discos around the world (next year it could be twenty!), and is a fantastic woman. She's got an electricity about her that just doesn't quit. I first met her when we did a TV show together in Los Angeles, and I liked her immediately—she's beautiful, sharp, affectionate and a great businesswoman with a sensational sense of humor. She tells a wonderful story about her first marriage. She was very young (about sixteen) and she kept telling her husband that she wanted to open her own club. Finally he sent her to a psychiatrist because he said she was "crazy." The marriage didn't last but her "crazy" dream of owning a club did, and grew till now she's the "Queen of Discos." She remarried and her very handsome husband of ten years, Roger Choukroun, is mad about her (and she about him). Regine has a drive to succeed that is exceeded only by her belief in her self, which is strengthened every day by each success.

    To like other people you have to like your self, and to like your self you have to believe in your self, and when you believe in your self you will like your self, and when you like your self you will like other people, and around it goes. So start to do some things, even little things, that will make you like yourself and will make you believe in yourself. Bake a beautiful cake, paint a picture of your house, join the Y or a health club and work out every day, write a poem about the love of your life (your husby, wife, roomie, dog, cat, turtle, plant, diamond bracelet), visit a veterans' hospital and watch some of the old vets' eyes light up because they haven't had a visitor for months or even years. A few years ago, when I first started acting, I decided to get some experience in front of an audience, so I memorized some monologues, called the Veterans' Hospital, and went out by myself to entertain. I was doing it solely to gain experience, not for any unselfish reasons. I was amazed that some of the men hadn't had any visitors for months, and they were terribly lonely. But one man was truly pathetic. He hadn't had one visitor for over twenty-five years and I just couldn't believe it. The nurses assured me it was true. This man had no living relatives, and no one cared if he lived or died. I was so moved by his loneliness that I spent a little extra time with him after my monologues. After we talked for a while, he asked me to excuse him for a minute, and went to another room, returning with a watercolor he had painted. He handed it to me and I could hardly control my emotions. The next week I wrote him a note thanking him for his gift, but I started the note out asking him if he remembered me (he was a very old man, in his nineties). I got a reply that I will never forget: "Do I rember you? You was like a angel come down from heaven." I was so touched that I began a correspondence that lasted for four years, until his death. I also visited him occasionally, and every time, he'd give me a new picture, which he'd painted for me. That experience, which started out as a selfish act to gain experience, was one of the most memorable of my life, and maybe the first glimmer of self-like that started in my life since childhood.

So you don't have to become President to start liking yourself. You can start with little things (like taking the shake and vites) and work your way up to jogging every morning, or cutting out smokes—whatever it is you start with, know that it'll absolutely make you start liking your self and believing in your self, and when that happens you'll know what life is *really* all about!

ISLE OF LOVE

CHAPTER

What Is My Source?

ONCE YOU GET relaxed *physically* via the milkshake, which leads to a relaxed *mental* attitude where you're thinking more clearly without negative distraction, which leads to a relaxed *emotional* life where you allow yourself to be a loving person —once you get to that point, you will allow your imagination to soar to all the positive possibilities floating around waiting to be grasped. After years of physical wreck-dom, mental torture and emotional stifling, with the help of the milkshake and vites I began to loosen up. It was a slow process but I hung in there. It took years to become a mental mess and it takes years to clear up the mess, but I knew I was on the right track. I sensed that every day as my body got less tense the rest of me—my mental and emotional life—was relaxing too. And I was eager for help from anyone or anything. I was reading a lot, looking for answers, and one day when I least expected it I met a woman who gave me one line which turned my head around completely. This happened a few years ago, when I was going through an emotional trauma and I was suffering terribly. The emotional pain was almost unbearable and after a few weeks of this awful suffering I met a woman who sensed that I needed help. I didn't tell her that I was suffering or what I was suffering about but we talked for a while, and then, out of the blue, she asked me if I knew that God is my Source. I can't explain exactly what happened to me mentally at that moment, but the thought of God's being my Source, the very essence of my being, crept into one of the crannies of my brain and hasn't left me to this day. I got a flash of an insight that if God *is* my Source (and I believe this to be true), then God which is Good which is Love can want only the best for me. And I suddenly realized that the terrible emotional pain that I was going through was really for my own good and growth to be a better person. Now I know you've all heard a zillion times someone say that something is for your own good (like when you were spanked as a kid), and I've heard this a zillion times too, but it didn't mean anything to me then. But when this woman said it I must have been ready for the depth of its meaning because from that moment the awful emotional pain passed and I *knew* I had grown and learned a lot through the experience, and I started to really trust my Source and understand that my Source really wants all the best things for me in this life and is leading me through different experiences so that I will get all the things I want. That trust started to grow and I began to sense and feel and know that everything that I needed was being sent to me so that I might change all the parts of me that I wanted and needed to change. When I say trust, I mean a deep and total trust that I am in Good Hands every day of my life. It started out strong when I first grabbed the thought, then it was up to me to make it stronger every day, and that's what I do.

Now everyone is different and something that impresses you won't necessarily impress me and vice-versa, but this one line went to the depths of my being. My Source—that's the very beginning, there is nothing beyond a source—and my Source is God or Good or Love (which are synonymous). For days it spun around in my head till it became etched in my brain. No matter what happens, that thought pops into my head. Now, when *any* kind of negative thought tries to cross my mind, I think, God is my Source, and I relax and that thought subconsciously takes over. The same way the vites and shake push out my need for coffee, cigs, etc., the thought of God as my Source pushes out negative thoughts. You can't just *not* think of a negative thought, you must replace it with a positive one (like you don't just stop drinking coffee, you replace it with the shake). Maybe a few weeks after I first got the thought, I started to think about it even more and realize that it could help me become what I wanted to become and to attain what I wanted to attain, so I hooked it onto the end of my slant-board physical exercises.

When I've finished my sit-ups, etc., I lie there and do some mental exercises and it's fun. I'm very relaxed after the physical exertion and can totally concentrate. I think, God is my Source, God is my only Source, God is my Source of everything. Then I softly say it aloud, and allow it to sink into my conscious and subconscious. Then I softly say, "I am forever relaxed and confident and self-reliant and energetic and having fun—God is my Source."

Most of us like to see immediate results when we do something. But some things take a little time. Now even if these mental exercises seem foolish to you and you don't think there's a chance they can work, do them. Even if you just do them by rote, your subconscious won't know the difference, so do them. Maybe you won't change the first day but after a while of doing them every day, you'll make a new groove in your brain (as I calls it) and before you know it, you'll have changed your whole life for the better. It takes all of two or three minutes, and it can change your life. It *will* change your life, but again, you must *do* them. The worst that can happen is you blow two minutes, and the best is you can change your whole life. Every time your conscious mind tells your subconscious mind something, it's etched there. And when you repeat it, it gets a little stronger, and after a while it gets so strong that it starts taking over your life. When good things start taking over your life, that's when you begin to enjoy life the way you're supposed to—with fun and pizazz. Life becomes a juicy feast laid out in front of you just waiting for you to taste all the different luscious flavors.

Each person makes up his or her own—whatever personal qualities are desirable, like self-confidence, self-reliance, relaxation, energy, fun. I say, "I am forever relaxed, and confident, self-reliant, energetic and having fun" (having fun is important to me—everything in life should be fun, or at least most things should, and can be, if we relax). To overcome certain weaknesses (which I don't want), I say, "I am the strongest person in the world—God is my Source" and "Love is always with me—God is my Source" and "My mind is open only to good —God is my Source." This relaxes me because I pass the responsibility from myself to my Giant Self (my Source). No longer do you have to worry about something happening—if it's right for you it will happen and your Source will take care of it, and if it isn't right for you, your Source will take care that it doesn't happen, at least at the moment . . . it may become right for you later. You don't have to worry about a thing. All you have to do is think of all the things you want in life and start working toward getting them, knowing that your Source is doing the real work.

Now I've been accused of being an Alfred E. Newman (What, me worry?) but those non-believers disbelieve anything they can't see, and of course they're also not believers in God or in the power of the subconscious. These exercises are all a form of self-hypnosis (the direct line of communication from the conscious to the subconscious), and science is daily proving the tremendous power of hypnosis.

Now I said if something isn't right for you, your Source will take care that it doesn't happen, but I don't mean that it won't ever happen. If you want something badly enough you may not get it right away, and it may seem like you're not going to get it at all, and that your Source isn't letting you have it because of some reason or something you did earlier that you think of as "bad," so your Source is punishing you by not letting you have what you want now. That is untrue and negative. If you *really* want something, and trust and love your Giant Self and know that your Giant Self (or call it your Source or God) really trusts and loves you, you will *know* that when the time is right you will get what you want. It may not be exactly what you want, but it will be the equivalent or better. For instance, if for ten years you've dreamed of owning your own home and you want a white house with red trim and a white picket fence around it, and you think about it and dream about it and work and save your money, and one day you're driving along a street and you see a yellow house with white trim and a redwood fence around it with a "For Sale" sign out front and it's a little more expensive than you'd been planning on, but you love it. So you borrow some extra money and you finally get a house. It's not exactly the house you've been thinking about, but you paint it white over the yellow, and the trim becomes red over the white, and you paint the redwood fence white, and now it's even more gorgeous and better than the one you were dreaming about.

If for whatever reason you've lost a love and you're torturing yourself with thoughts that you'll never find another love as fulfilling as this lost one, know in your heart that you not only will find an-

other love, but the next one will be even more fulfilling than the one you lost. You lost this love because
you needed to grow and you weren't growing in
that situation (and maybe he or she wasn't either).
Believe me, when a love situation is really terrific on
both sides, it grows daily, and both of you grow
daily as individuals, and the relationship grows
stronger. In the big picture of our journey through
life, we must realize that we are here to grow and
become more loving (lack of growth means a stifling
of love).

In the last few years a question has really been
bothering me. I began to realize that the basis of all
unhappiness is fear. Now lots of people think that
hate or envy or jealousy are the negative bases of
unhappiness, but none of these negatives could or
would exist without fear. But where does fear come
from? Everything has to have a beginning, a cause.
And if God, or Love, or Spirit, or Source, or Giant
Self, is *everything,* then how could something negative like fear exist? But more important to me,
where does fear *begin?* This question has haunted
me for years and I didn't have a clue what the answer was. Then, the other day (while I was writing
this chapter), I had lunch with a business acquaint-
ance whom I like and admire very much. He's a very
sweet, calm, loving man but he'd told me several
months before that he used to be a more driving,
pushy person, until he had found inner peace
through his wife's religion. I didn't go into it at the
time because I thought it would be a sticky "religious" kind of conversation (which to me means talk
about churches and outward appearances of good,

but seldom the real thing of kindness and love in action). But my curiosity got the better of me at lunch, so I asked him exactly what had happened to bring about this change in himself. And he gave me a quotation from the Bible that he said was important to him: "God giveth us not a spirit of fear, but of power, of love, and of a sound mind." At that very moment, the whole question of fear was answered for me in a flash of insight. I suddenly understood clearly where fear comes from. When a person knows God and feels the presence of Love and understands that Giant Self adores him or her and wants only the best, then fear cannot exist. But when you don't know and feel Love, there is a void, and a void must be filled (a void is a vacuum and you all know what happens in a vacuum—how it sucks in everything around it). When Love isn't in your mind, fear must be, because fear is the absence of Love (or God, or Spirit, or Source, or Giant Self).

So, every time a fear thought invades your mind, just relax (and you'll be able to if you're taking the shake and vites every day), and concentrate on knowing that your Source adores you and is guiding you in every way and wants you to be happy and loving and having fun.

I believe—no, I am certain—that there is a direct ratio between love and fear in a person's life. The more love you keep in your mind, the less fear can lodge there. And the more fear that permeates your thinking, the less love will exist in your life. If eighty percent of your conscious mind is steeped in anger and jealousy and fear, then only twenty percent of your mind can express love. But by making a conscious effort to change the percentage through self-hypnosis, you can change it to seventy percent fear and thirty percent love. And with more effort and conscious will, you can change it to sixty percent fear and forty percent love, and so on, until you tip the scales in the other direction.

But it is a direct ratio. And to change it you don't concentrate on getting rid of the fear (which only makes the fear more real), but you do concentrate on thinking and expressing kindness to your self and to others. That pushes out the thoughts of fear and their expressions. If you start to concentrate, "God is my Source," and keep that thought ever handy and push it in whenever a fear thought creeps up, eventually it will become a habit and will automatically jump in when you need it. When the temptation is strongest to tense up and be fearful (like when I haven't got the bank payment and I'm already a month late and the man at the bank said okay so long as I have two payments next month and I promised I would and something happened and I don't have it and I'm really upset), I find that knowing that God is my Source calms me down and allows me to think clearly about how and where to come up with the money (fear and tension make it more difficult to think clearly).

After you've done this a few times, it gets easier. Like everything else, the more you do something, the more of a habit it becomes and you automatically begin to do it without thinking. So try to catch yourself when *any* kind of fear thought comes into your mind, and immediately relax your body and think of your Source which is only good and loving and is taking great care of you. I mean, with something as powerful as your Giant Self looking out for you, how could anything but good things happen to you?

When you realize that religion is something inside you and not a building or statues or anything outside you, then you begin to realize how truly powerful it is. When you're working with your subconscious (and you have to quiet your conscious mind, or forebrain thinking, before your subconscious can really get to work), that's when your life begins to change. This was probably the hardest thing for me to learn. I was mostly forebrain thinking (and full of fear, envy, anger, hate, and all those ugly negatives), and I was most unhappy. Only when I began to realize that I was responsible for most of the unhappy experiences in my life, and the few happy moments seemed to come when I was relaxed and not trying to control my life, did real change come about. When I learned that the only thing I have to control is my feeling of love which in turn fills my being and keeps out fear, that's when the moments of happiness started to outnumber the awful fears and other negs.

Dr. Curt G. Batiste, a psychiatrist, believes that those who believe in God are happier and have less stress and tensions, and are much healthier than non-believers. When a person prays, that prayer is a form of positive thinking, and positive thinking makes our immunity systems stronger. Dr. Batiste says that four out of five of his psychiatric patients are not what you would call religious people, and he believes that those who are religious are less likely to look for psychiatric help.

How about if we turn around "prayer is positive thinking" to "positive thinking is prayer"? We tend to think of prayer as some mumbo-jumbo words usually said in a church or temple, but if prayer is positive thinking, then it follows that positive thinking is definitely prayer. And the more positive your thoughts are, the closer to God, Love, Spirit, Giant Self or Source you are.

Donny and Marie Osmond are very fortunate that they have such an outstanding and loving mother. Olive Osmond is a woman bursting with love and she daily expresses it. Thirty years ago Mrs. Osmond discovered that her oldest sons, Tom and Virl, had an almost complete hearing loss, and of course she was terribly upset, but she refused to despair. She has such a love and trust in life and God that she believed she was specially chosen to be the mother of these handicapped little boys, and she knew she had to do something herself to help them with their hearing problems. Mrs. Osmond had been a schoolteacher, so she went out and got all the literature and information she could on deafness. She worked hours each day with each boy to help them learn to talk. She bought records with different sounds on them and Tom and Virl would practice making noises and sounds and then making up what the noises meant and putting them in scrapbooks. They would cut out pictures and put printed captions underneath them, paste them in the books and then work with the sounds. Both boys learned sign language at school, but when they came home their mother insisted that they talk. Then, when her other kids started to study singing, she called a dance teacher and the boys took lessons in tap dancing. She insisted they learn to play the saxophone, and it was loud enough for them to feel the vibrations so they could "hear" the noises they were making on them. Mrs. Osmond is remarkable in her love and determination, but I believe it was her enormous love that led to her determination.

While I was jogging on my "jogging machine" the other day (it's not actually a machine but a 20 × 22-inch piece of foam rubber with springs, covered with vinyl, and slanted up so it's like running uphill), I got my imagination going and came up with a thought about fear. I run on my jogger every day and I never look down or think about falling off it (it's about four inches off the ground). If I were standing on a 20 × 22-inch platform ten feet high or fifty feet high or a hundred feet high, I'd be so scared I wouldn't even be able to stand—I'd probably sit on it and hang onto the sides for dear life with the fear of falling off making me so petrified I'd be shaking. But when it's four inches high I run on it for many minutes, never look down, and never even consider falling off. Whenever I start imagining running on it if it were fifty feet high, the thought is so scary that I'm sure I'd fall off, even if I just stood still. That's what fear does to you—and me. It tenses you up and makes you totally negative, and probably makes whatever you fear happen (like your fear would *make* you fall off the jogger fifty feet high).

I wanted to test out my fear theory so a few days ago, while being examined by a gynecologist, I de-

cided to see if it worked. Now, usually, I'm the
biggest chicken in the world at the doctor's office.
For instance, it's pathetic to see me giving blood.
First I can't look at the tube or bottle (I told you I'm
a chicken) and I usually sing to keep my mind occu-
pied, and of course I'm very tense during the process. Anytime I think something will hurt, I always
warn the doctor (or dentist) ahead of time (so I won't
surprise him or her too much when the moment of
truth arrives). I always tell all of them that I am a
chicken, that I was born a chicken and that pain has
a really extreme effect on me—in fact, just the
thought of pain gets me pretty nervous. I've been
going through my act since I was a little kid, and
even though it's embarrassing for a grown person
like me to be so scared, I figured it must go back to
some awful physical trauma when I was a baby or
something, and the fear of pain must have left its
indelible mark, so I've always accepted my chicken-
ness. Well, anyway, there I was on the table, ready
for the exam but very tense, and the doctor told me
to relax. My fear theory popped into my head and
I thought, okay, kid, it's now or never. I told my
body to relax . . . and it did—then I immediately
thought of my Source who adores me and wants me
to have everything I want (including no pain), and
my mind actually kept the thought so strong that I
stayed relaxed. I was able to push out the fear-
thought (because the exam really doesn't hurt, but
I was always waiting for it to hurt—I was expecting
pain, I was thinking hard about pain, so no wonder
I used to be tense). It was a terrific feeling to know
that for the first time in my life *I* controlled my

mind under the pressure of expecting pain. I concentrated so much on relaxing that there wasn't room for fear.

These mental and emotional exercises are the beginning of a person's real strength. The stronger you feel mentally and emotionally, the more you can allow your Source to take over and run your life. When we're weak, we're fearful, and we really screw up our lives by trying to control everything. It's like when an IBM machine is programmed wrong and the machine jams. That's what happens to our brains (mental machines). Thoughts of fear tense us up, and all that tension constricts our bodies, paralyzes our emotions, and jams our minds. When this happens, there's no way our subconscious or our Source or Giant Self can lead us.

So, to allow our strengths to grow, we must use them. Self-discipline is a tremendous teacher. Through the years I've worked on myself to become stronger and it's working—gradually, but working. Once in a while, just to test myself, I'll make myself do something really difficult. When I'm eating something scrumptious, something I *really* like, I'll wonder if I can make myself stop—so about two-thirds of the way through, when I'm still hungry and super-enjoying the food, I make myself put down the fork or spoon and just stop eating. I'll look at the food and know that I'm the master. (If you think it's easy, try it! Now it's got to be something you really *love* to eat, something that makes you salivate just to think of it.) The feeling of power and strength is tremendous when you know that you are the master of your world. To be strong is to feel

invincible—and to feel the power of your Source or
Giant Self working within you. And you feel good
when you feel strong. I mean good in every way—
a sense of well-being, and a sense that you are a good
person. Bette Davis once said something very perceptive:

> "The weak are the most treacherous of all. It's the
> strong who are vulnerable."

Or as Leo Rosten put it:

> "It's the weak who are cruel. Gentleness can only be
> expected from the strong."

That's so true. To be weak is to be fearful, and
when you're fearful you're tense and treacherous
and angry and hostile and jealous. To be strong is
to be relaxed, and when you're relaxed you're open
and trusting and warm and loving and vulnerable—
and when you think positively, you can only be
vulnerable to good.

Mohammed Ali is one of my all-time favorite people. Behind his bravado and humor lurks a heart so
full of love that it just knocks me out (!). His big
project now is an organization called WORLD—
World Organization for Rights, Liberty and Dig-
nity—which is an international service foundation.
He believes that everything in life has a purpose—
trees have a purpose, pigs have a purpose, termites
have a purpose—and he says that man, who is God's
greatest creation, has a purpose too. Ali believes that
"service to others is the rent we pay for our room

in heaven," and he has such a strong belief in God
that it is the moving force in his life. He says that
his main thing is to serve God, that his ministry, like
Oral Roberts' and Billy Graham's, is the most important thing in the world to him, and that world
evangelism is his goal. Now *that's* a religious man—
not in the church-going sense, but in the real sense
of trying to do good for others and having a strong
belief in the goodness of himself and others.

Shaun Cassidy knows that his Source is love and
he's a very together person. According to Shaun, all
this is due to his mother, Shirley Jones, who gave
him and his two younger brothers lots of love mixed
with discipline. Shirley is a great lover of everything, including music and people, and this has
rubbed off on Shaun. I worked with Shaun's father,
actor and singer Jack Cassidy, and we became good
friends before his tragic, untimely death several
years ago. Jack was crazy about his kids, and when
he and Shirley split he was shattered and never
pulled out of his emotional tailspin. He was a fine
actor and a terrific friend, but he couldn't get himself all together. His childhood was not a happy one
and his ego was constantly begging for approval
because of this. But Shaun has been raised in a different world, and with Shirley's help and guidance
and enormous capacity for love, he has his physical,
mental and emotional life much more together than
his father, and has a surprisingly mature outlook on
everything. He says that acting and singing and
performing are okay for now, but eventually he
wants to be a producer. Shaun definitely knows
where he's going.

Former President Gerald Ford's vivacious wife Betty says, "Life begins at sixty." Just before she hit that birthday, she was heavily into liquor and drugs, and after a family confrontation that was both necessary and traumatic, she checked into a hospital and announced publicly that she was addicted to alcohol and tranquilizers. Since that time she hasn't touched either one, and she says she feels better at sixty than she's ever felt. Betty has a strong belief in God, and that belief has given her the strength to cope with tremendous pressures. She temporarily fell into the trap of thinking that drugs (booze and pills) can help a person to cope, but when she finally realized that she was fooling no one with her slurring speech, her stumbling and her failing memory, she pulled herself together. She says that with God's help she overcame it all and made a beautiful comeback, which made her husband, her children and herself very proud and happy.

When you know that your Source is God (or Spirit, or Love, or your Giant Self or whatever you want to call It/Her/Him), you'll feel such a sense of power that it'll amaze you. As Shakespeare said, "There is nothing either good or bad, but thinking makes it so." So think, feel, KNOW that your Source is working for you, and the power of your Source will become *your* power.

CHAPTER

Who Adores Me?

BEING LOVED IS just as important as loving, because in order to love, the lover must have a *lovee*. It takes two to love unless you're a masochist on the non-receiving end of a one-sided love affair (as that great lyricist Larry Hart said, "Unrequited love's a bore"). I think it's more painful than boring, but according to all the stories about Hart, his love affairs were *all* unrequited, so after a few it probably did become boring.

Just as loving is an art, being loved is also an art. It can be learned and coaxed into growing. It's like giving and receiving—most people know how to give (even though they may not do it all the time), but many people honestly don't know how to receive. They get embarrassed when someone gives them something. Watch a person when he or she receives a compliment and see if it embarrasses him or her. It seems as if lots of us don't feel we deserve the gift or the compliment. I know I used to stutter out a denial if someone complimented me: "Oh, it's not a new dress, I've had it for ages," or, "My mother's got better legs than I," or "I think everybody looks great with a tan." I wasn't able to accept that someone really liked something about me—I didn't feel I was worth very much, so they obviously must be mistaken or putting me on—and I was embarrassed.

It took me a long time to figure out how to overcome this. First I had to start thinking better about myself, and even though that sounds easy when you say it fast, it was extremely difficult for me to do. I guess it depends on how nothing you think you are —if you figure you're okay, not sensational but at least okay, well, that's one thing. But if you see yourself as worthless, then you've got a huge job in front of you.

One day, after I'd made a particularly ridiculous scene mumbling some sort of a denial about a compliment I'd just been given, I was very upset with myself and sat down and made a last-ditch effort to figure out how to get over this. I tried to figure out why I carried this awful guilt around, this conviction that I didn't deserve compliments. And it went much further than that—the guilt affected every area of my life. I searched my memory to see whether it had started with my parents or relatives (I distinctly remembered at the age of six, sitting at our dining room table and a visitor telling my aunt how pretty I was and my aunt getting all upset and telling the woman never to say that again. Because I now know my aunt meant well, I don't *think* the guilt started there). Then I tried to remember if something in particular ever happened in the religious school I went to for twelve years (of course they always teach that rich people are somehow not as good as poor people and you shouldn't strive for pleasure—pain seems to get you into heaven faster, and poverty almost assures it; maybe the guilt did start there because I sure never wanted to be poor and suffering). Well, I spent hours probing my exhausted mind, and because I'm very logical (I'm also full of feeling which proves to *me* that you can have both, or to put it another way, can be both logical and emotional at the same time), I came up with some terrific thoughts and ideas, which helped me immensely.

I knew that it was always easier for me to love than be loved, so I decided to start with that. My guilt (or something) kept me from feeling worthy of being loved. It was relatively easy for me to find someone who I felt was terrific and love him or her, but because I didn't feel I was so hot, I didn't feel worthy of being loved by others.

So I came up with an emotional exercise that I have done every day since that day, and it's made the biggest change in my emotional life than anything else, so that now I'm beginning to be able to accept compliments and just say, "Thank you."

Every morning, at the end of my physical and mental slant-board exercises, I do my emotional exercises. I just lie there and close my eyes and totally relax. Then I remember emotionally what it was like when someone *really* loved me (mother, father, husband, wife—it makes no difference who, but you must remember the *feeling* of being loved, the wonderful physical glow and warmth and open feeling of someone truly loving you). This takes real concentration and you must be relaxed, but it's really fun. When I've captured this warm feeling, I smile and say, "God adores me," and then I smile bigger and keep that great feeling of openness and warmth. Then I say, "God adores me and wants me to have *everything* I want." Now, follow my logic—assuming that God, or Love, or Giant Self exists, and *really* loves me (which we've been taught mentally but not emotionally), It (She/He) certainly wants me to have everything. My darling mother wants me to have everything she can give me; when my father was alive he loved me dearly and wanted me to have anything and everything my little heart desired. So God, who *adores* me (I like the word "adore" better than "love" in this case because it seems stronger to me to emotionally capture the feeling. But you can use love or cherish or any word that works for you), wants me to have everything in the whole world that I want.

Now I get into a little more detail. "God adores me and wants me to have everything I want"— usually I keep to that, but once in a while I list all the things I want (and you pick all the things you've ever really wanted and realize that if God *does* adore you, you'll get all these terrific things—success, love, friends, money, a great job, a terrific apartment you can afford, beautiful clothes, fame, a new car, a diamond ring, a baby). Whoever really loved you would have given you *anything* you wanted, and if God adores you and you not only believe it but you *feel* it, the feeling will daily grow till you feel more and more loved, and you feel more and more deserving of everything you want. It's very important to smile broadly, because that'll help you to feel loved and happy.

As I said before, my biggest problem was that I never felt I deserved anything. I felt only guilty for wanting good things for myself. Again, maybe it was my religious upbringing with Hell and guilt, etc., or maybe it came from somewhere else, but it was there, coloring everything I did. No wonder I repelled myself from getting good things from my life—I didn't feel I deserved them. But doing this *every day,* and without exception, makes me know I'm loved and feel like I'm a lovable person who deserves everything I want. Feeling loved makes you realize the goodness within yourself, which is your REAL SELF or "My Giant Self," as I call God.

It's terrific to feel adorable, and I'll tell you how this feeling led me to something utterly fantastic. Up until the time I started doing this emotional exercise, I'd never owned anything of real value. Oh, sure, I'd owned cars and furniture for apartments, and a little jewelry and a couple of fur coats (this was before I became aware of how much I love animals and stopped wearing fur and, as a lot of you know, also stopped eating meat. This, as I explained in my "Energy" book, has nothing to do with meat not being good for you and a protein, but only because I have a thing about killing animals), but I'd never had anything *really* valuable. I'd thought a lot about owning a house, but the kind of house I envisioned seemed totally out of the question. Well, several years ago, when I started my "God adores me and wants me to have everything I want" routine, I started to read the New York *Times* Sunday real estate section and sort of browse through it. After a few weeks of having fun dreaming about living in some of these places, one ad in particular caught my eye. It was a penthouse co-op with a wrap-around terrace. Now I must explain that when I was a very little kid I fell madly in love with New York City without ever having been there. I grew up on the West Coast, but dreamed of living in Manhattan. It probably started with those wonderful old movies with gorgeous penthouses and a very sophisticated sensuous-looking woman in a slinky gown seducing the marvelous-looking fella in white tie and tails on the terrace, each with a glass of champagne, and looking out over the skyline of all those great buildings that make up Manhattan. Anyway, the ad listed a woman's name and phone number. I called the number and found out the woman was a broker. I told her I was interested in seeing the co-op (now mind you, I didn't have a cent to my name—oh, I had enough to pay the rent and buy my yeast and lecithin and vites, and dog and cat and turtle food for Seymour and Nathan and Oswald, but nothing else). Anyway, we set up an appointment and the next day we met in front of a beautiful building on Manhattan's East Side. The broker took me up, and as soon as I got inside the apartment, I fell in love with it. I envisioned all the changes I would make

—I was already knocking out walls, adding partitions, planting a glorious, HUGE terrace with maple trees and petunias. I was in heaven making my plans. She told me the price (which was astronomical—listen, as long as I was dreaming, I might as well dream *big*), and I (being a great actress) said I'd have to think about it. She asked me if I'd like to see any more apartments, and I said sure. She had no idea how much fun I was having. So in the next few weeks she called me a few times and showed me some more palatial co-ops, all of them tremendously expensive. She was awfully nice so I decided to tell her I didn't even have a fraction of the down payment, but that some day I knew I would. She was darling about it (by now we were becoming friends) and said yes, she believed that some day I would too, and in the meantime she would just love to continue showing me fabulous places. Every once in a while, when she found a particularly spectacular apartment, she would call me and we'd go look and I was just having a marvelous time. My imagination was working overtime in furnishing the places and it was really fun.

Several years went by and we kept in touch and she continued showing me places, and one day I called her and said I had finally accumulated a little bread (not a lot, but more than I had before), and I'd like to start looking in earnest for something I could afford. So we kept at it and one autumn day I found IT, the place I'd always wanted. It was literally love at first sight and I wrote out a small check for a deposit to hold it. I knew I didn't have nearly enough for the down payment, so I figured out how

I could borrow enough to make it. I called a close friend and he borrowed from several of *his* friends, enough for me to get my place (now *there's* a friend!). So my new friend the real estate agent made her commission because she believed in me, and I got my house because I dared to dream that one day I could own it. (I'm still paying back the down payment and will be paying the mortgage for many years, but I *love* it!)

It's so terrific to aspire to something and so awful and dull and boring not to. That's one thing I don't like about communism and socialism. I lived in Copenhagen for almost ten months while making a TV pilot film, *The Green Eyed Elephant* (which didn't sell) and a TV movie *Operation Camel,* which now plays every once in a while on the tube. Anyway, Copenhagen is a gorgeous city with beautiful scenery, friendly people, great food (it's known as the "Paris of the North") and a lot of fun. But it is socialistic—there are no real rich and no real poor. It sounds terrific but it doesn't work out so terrific. Because you can't ever get rich or ever become a star or a millionaire, no one aspires to anything. I remember an actor turning down a lead in a film because it conflicted with his holiday. And when they called a coffee-break mid-morning, the entire crew would have schnapps and Tuborg—at 10:00 in the morning! If you can't aspire, life is dull, and alcohol relieves the boredom.

I've always tried to better myself and my life, and believe me, I've come a long way—and I've still got a ways to go. I used to be the most insecure, negative person (of course a lot of it was because I was a tense person physically from childhood on). I not only had to overcome my insecurity, fears, negativism, etc., but I had the nerve to aspire to good things. Like I said, when I was a kid growing up I watched all the movies about New York (and now my all-time favorite movie has become Woody Allen's *Manhattan*—I've only seen it six times!) and secretly fell in love with the Big Apple. I knew I'd eventually wind up here, and I did. I aspired to star in films and I am (true, they aren't *Gone With the Wind*, but I'm still aspiring). It's amazing how things come to pass when you make your wishes known to yourself and start thinking about them, and then have the guts to let other people know what you want.

When I was living in Hollywood and just starting in acting, people would usually ask me what did I like about acting and why did I want to be an actor. I always came up with the same line—"I just want to express human feeling through other people's experiences" (I must have read that somewhere—I couldn't have created those lines myself). Then I'd go into "all I want is to be a good actress—fame means nothing to me, and the money is unimportant." I was very poor at the time and I guess it would have been embarrassing to let people know money was important, because then they'd wonder about how dumb I must be to want it and be so poor —this way it gave me an out. My excuse was I really didn't care for money—I enjoyed struggling. . . .

As I matured mentally and got more honest with myself, I realized what a crock all that was. *Nobody* enjoys being poor, and it's one thing to kid other people, but it's really stupid to kid yourself. So I analyzed myself and realized I want to be a super-star multimillionaire, and for a few years now I've been telling *everyone* that that's what I want to be. Lots of people kid me about it (I'm known to some as "SS" and to some others as "SSMM"), but after years of hiding my desire from myself and from others, and of being embarrassed about wanting great things, and, of course, of thinking I wasn't worthy of wanting them, this feels terrific. And my subconscious keeps hearing it so it keeps getting stronger and more deeply etched in my brain. It's again a form of self-hypnosis (the more I say it, the more I believe it). I'm sure Mohammed Ali used the same idea when he used to say "I'm the greatest" and "I'm pretty"—and the idea worked because he believed it and eventually *did* become the greatest!

There have been rumors that all the airlines may rip out first-class sections and have all one-class flying, and I, for one, hope it never happens. Even when I was a pauper (not so long ago), I loved to dream about flying first class (plus doing all those other terrific expensive things like wearing designer clothes or having a chauffered limousine). Good grief, if we're all alike and dress alike, what a total bore! I love aspiring to different things. Now I may never *have* a Rolls Royce with a chauffeur or a maid to serve my milkshake in bed and take care of me, but it sure is fun to dream about. And I'd hate to think that all those goodies didn't exist. The only thing that's sad is when people *don't* aspire because of fear or the negative thought that something is impossible. *Nothing is impossible.* Anything you can imagine (image-in) you can attain. It may take great discipline and determination and years of hard work, but when the vision of attainment is before you, you work without complaining. Just the thought of having what you dream about is exciting.

One of the most important faculties we all have is our memory. We use it every minute of our lives. We remember how to get up, brush our teeth, make our shake and take our vites. That's how things become habits. We remember them and they become second nature after we've done them a few times. So without our memory we really couldn't do anything. If every time were the first time, we never would have left the jungle. We'd still be scrounging for food (every day our hunger would tell us to get food and every day we'd have to figure out how and where) and dodging tigers. But we have another faculty just as important as our memory, but in a different way. Without this function, we wouldn't accomplish much, but the sad part is, not many of us use it. All successful people do though, because without it everyone would be discouraged and would give up. What I'm talking about is our "forgettory." Just as we have to remember certain things, we also have to forget certain things. As children we tried to walk and we fell. We tried to eat with a spoon and we slopped up everything. As we grew, we continued trying and temporarily failing, and if we'd remembered the failures, we never would have continued trying. The same with now. If you don't try, you'll get nothing. But if you do try, you must realize that trial and error is the only way to succeed. I've tried lots and lots of things. In fact, I'm always trying something new. I succeed sometimes, and I fail a lot. Failing doesn't make a person a failure. Failure is an attitude, but failing is a good sign that someone is trying (like they said when I was in grammar school—"That's what erasers are for"). When I try to accomplish something, I consciously use my forgettory to forget every failure, and I remember only my successes. Otherwise I'd be disheartened and give up. I believe I'll win because that's the only message I allow in my brain —that I'll succeed. All the negative thoughts of my previous failures are quickly and consciously and deliberately forgotten. You know you can "will" anything. You can choose to do whatever you feel is best. And if you love yourself (and see yourself as an extension of your Source or Giant Self), how can you focus on anything *but* your successes?

So many of us will not to feel because we're afraid of our feelings, but this closes us off from the basics of life. How we felt about something is what it is to us. Dr. Robert Kronemeyer wrote a sensational article, published in *Psychotherapy: Theory, Research and Practice*, which is a national professional journal read by doctors, students, and lay people interested in clinical psychology. The article is entitled "Syntonic Therapy: A Total Approach to the Treatment of Mental and Emotional Disturbances".

> The word "syntony" refers to a harmonious arrangement of parts into a whole; in this instance, the body, mind, emotions, and spirit of the patient becoming re-unified into a more physically relaxed, reasonable, emotionally secure and spiritually alive Self.
> Through mis-education, modern man lost much of

the aliveness and flowing spontaneity with which he was created; the stream becomes dammed up in pathological tension, and occasionally breaks out in destructive violence in individuals or en masse.

This emotional plague cripples human will, twists love into fear and hostility, and frustrates the human potential for responsibility, maturity, and happiness. Because of this state of the human condition, new therapies endeavor to find ways of reaching the whole person in order to restore the capacity to be a total Self —capable of feeling—thinking—choosing—acting—being—in creative ways.

It is important to warn the patient that he will feel both worse and better, as he begins to feel again, so he is less likely to run at the first hint of panic or rage. I also explain that drugs and alcohol are antitherapeutic and suggest a program of healthy nutrition, rest and exercise. After the first session, a relationship has begun, the mutual responsibilities understood (the patient responsible for freeing himself with my help) and the goals of the person clarified.

The next step with the patient who is cut off from feeling and wants deep personality change, rather than counseling or temporary support, is to introduce what I call "the language of emotion." Before we used words, we all expressed ourselves in infancy and early childhood through sounds and movements, our primary non-verbal language. The deepest emotions in life are "beyond words." Accordingly I hand the patient a large rolled-up towel—negative emotions must be noisy if fully expressed. Frequently just making sounds will loosen some of the stoppages of the mind (repression) and of the chronic visceral and more surface muscular tensions. Sounds trigger emotions for another reason, beside the fact that they were the language of our infancy and re-kindle buried feelings, memories and experiences. In order to make sounds one must increase respiration! All disturbed persons, being both anxious and tense, tend to hold their breath as a natural part of the fear reaction. They find it impossible to relax and "draw a free breath" because of watchfulness and chronically tense muscles.

Re-gaining the freedom which is one's birthright, and the capacity for flowing, loving and constructively assertive feelings which are essential for self-esteem, emotional health, and rational living, requires power. Of the three negative emotions: fear-panic-terror, sadness-hopelessness-despair, and annoyance-anger-rage, only the latter has the outgoing energy necessary to overcome the tenacious self-defeating patterns.

Gradually the patient becomes aware of being frustrated at his painful state of fear and tension. Encouraged by the positive alliance with the therapist as well as his own desire to avoid pain and achieve pleasure, and being confronted with the fact that now only he is keeping himself crippled, he becomes angry. Aggressive movements such as kicking, hitting the couch, twisting the towel, usually come spontaneously out of this frustration.

Increased resistance must be dealt with on a conceptual level. As the original images of the pathogenic family come into awareness, the fear, rage and guilt that prompted the patient to build the character and muscular armor in the first place break through. I now explain to patients that everyone has mixed feelings about their parents—loved the "good" parents, pitied the "weak" parents, feared and hated the "bad" parents.

I assert the patient's right to do whatever they wish,

not to their actual parents, but to the inner images of their parents! Since they created these images, they have the right to destroy them, or any part of them that they wish!

Fear, rage and sadness in varying degrees thrive in every human being of any age to the extent that they have lost inner security and the capacity to feel pleasure and love.

The transition from fear and guilt, through rage, to love, understanding and compassion is beautiful to see. When the person is no longer emotionally crippled, the capacity for forgiveness comes into being.

Every problem has a solution—I firmly believe this—and that goes for every emotional problem too. You may have to probe for it, but it's there, waiting to be discovered. You may find the shake and vites are the entire solution, or you may need outside help to go with them. There are many fine therapists, psychiatrists, analysts, etc., and there are some not-so-fine, so if you don't feel the first one you meet is right, keep asking and looking until you find one you really groove with and feel comfortable and easy talking to. With the right person helping you, you'll be on your way to accepting yourself, which leads to liking yourself, which is the first step to happiness.

Back to the feeling of being adored—it's super-sensational and you don't even need someone around to do it. If you can recapture that wonderful feeling of warmth and openness and relaxation (it must be the feeling we had when we were infants and were totally taken care of), then you can feel adored all the time. And let's face it—it sure beats feeling rejected or disliked! So get your feelings warmed up and in action, so you can feel loved and adored now, while waiting for someone else to discover how sensational you are—and others will find out, because it's impossible to feel terrific about yourself without other people picking up on it. If you love your self, very shortly lots of other people are going to too!

CHAPTER 6

Love Is a Four Letter Word

ISLE OF VIEW . . . I love you . . .

If my book has done nothing but gotten people to say, "I love you," it will have done a lot.

I love your coat . . . I like you.

I love that house . . . I like you.

I loved that new movie . . . I like you.

I love your red hair and green eyes . . . I like you.

Let's start *loving* each other.

Just because I love you doesn't mean we have to get married. Just because you tell me you love me doesn't mean I've got the house all picked out. Love is a commitment, yes, but not a contract. It's a commitment to treat each other beautifully, to be warm and caring, not to hurt.

Loving takes the guts to be vulnerable, not to have

to hit back after you are hurt (and that's not easy). Love is caring enough to say "I'm sorry." I never could figure out the movie *Love Story* and the ad campaign for it. How can love be never having to say you're sorry? If you love someone and hurt him or her—and it happens to all of us, each and every one, the hurting and being hurt—a genuine "I'm sorry" dissolves the hurt. No matter how awful the blunder or oversight or slight, a sincere "I'm sorry" will erase it. When you say I'm sorry and the person knows you mean it, hostility vanishes. No matter how mad you are at someone's stupidity, which caused you pain or cost you money, if you feel the person is genuinely sorry, you will forget it. You can't stay angry at a truly sorry person because you feel "he's like me—we all make mistakes." Being sorry is empathy, feeling into another's feelings and expressing sorrow for hurting.

Lots of people seem to be emotionally constricted when it comes to love. I know I used to be. When I was very young I was so afraid of pain that I locked myself inside a protective emotional cocoon so that no one could hurt me. And no one did because I didn't allow it. I had superficial relationships that were very unsatisfying physically, mentally and emotionally. Slowly, as my awareness grew, I realized that life is feeling, and if you close yourself off from feeling because of a fear of being hurt, you close yourself off from life. So I very gradually started shedding the layers of protective gauze and started experiencing the true joy of life as I learned to love and be loved. Sure, I got hurt lots of times, but the joy of openness far outweighed the pain.

As for pain—why is it we always think our own problems are the worst anyone ever experienced? And why do we always feel we're the only person going through a trauma? It ain't so, believe me—and when you realize that everyone, without exception, experiences emotional pain and lives through it, it will lessen your own pain. Just knowing that other people have suffered like you are suffering, that right now, at the very moment of your suffering, there are thousands of people, maybe hundreds of thousands, who have lost a wife, a husband, a lover, a child, and this loss is overwhelming them, but as my all-time favorite philosopher, Ralph Waldo Emerson, said:

"Time and I against all things."

As time passes, so does the pain. Oh, you may never forget the suffering, but that awful gut-wrenching hurt lessens as days become months. Sure, you'll get a twinge when you think about it, but the tears won't come as quickly and the nausea will begin to subside so you can start eating right again once you put a little time under your belt. I have found that when I'm at my lowest, in the pits, I start to expect things to brighten up. That's when a new deal comes along—or a new love.

The first time I read *The Prophet* by Kahlil Gibran I was astounded by the beauty and the logic of it. One of the lines that I never forgot was:

The deeper that sorrow carves into your being, the more joy you can contain.

That's been so true in my life. When I was scared of being hurt and kept myself closed off, I never experienced the real joy of love. And now that I'm becoming more open, I'm more vulnerable to pain, but I now know that love is more important than all the sorrow in the world.

Another Gibran quote that I love is:

Some of you say, "Joy is greater than sorrow," and others say, "Nay, sorrow is the greater." But I say unto you, they are inseparable. Together they come, and when one sits alone with you at your board, remember that the other is asleep upon your bed.

Whenever I'm in the middle of some trauma, I think of these words and so far I've always found them true for me. They keep me from getting too high and too low. In my moments of sorrow I know that soon joy will find me and when I'm bursting with happiness I know that sorrow will again touch me. And why shouldn't it be that way? I can honestly say that I've learned most of the important things in my life during the moments of sorrow. When I'm happy I'm floating along on my happiness. But when I'm in emotional pain, I introspect and probe my thoughts and feelings and come up with answers to how to become a better person—better to myself and better to others—and therefore a happier person.

Nobel Prize-winner Isaac Bashevis Singer, a rabbi's son from Warsaw who immigrated to America in 1935, is one of the world's most prolific writers. He's a journalist, memoirist, novelist, playwright and children's storyteller. The central idea in all his works is that no one should ever belittle any emotion, or feeling. He says that the philosophers all belittled the emotions, especially Spinoza; who taught that all emotions were evil. Singer believes that everything that goes through our minds, no matter how silly or trivial, and no matter how terrible, is of some value. He says if you take away the emotions from a human being, that no matter how much logic he might have he will be a vegetable —the emotions and the man are the same. And he's especially interested in the emotions that become passions. Mr. Singer was interviewed in the New York *Times* by Laurie Colwin and he told her that he agrees with what Spinoza says in his *Ethics,* that everything in life can become a passion, especially if it has anything to do with sex or with the supernatural, because sex and the supernatural are very much the same. He feels that the need that human beings feel for each other is not only a physical need but also a need of the soul. Two people—a man and woman, two men, or two women—when embracing and saying they can't live without each other and feeling a mad, passionate, crazy desire for each other are not just experiencing a physical thing, it's much, much more than physical.

And Bertrand Russell says in *Marriage and Morals,*

I believe myself that romantic love is the source of the most intense delights that life has to offer.

There was a terrific article in *Family Health* magazine by Elizabeth Kaye, called "Warning: Falling in Love May Be Hazardous to Your Health."

Are you now, or have you ever been, hopelessly head over heels in love?

If so, according to Professor Dorothy Tennov, a behavioral psychologist and professor of psychology at the University of Bridgeport in Connecticut, who has just completed ten years of research in the field of romantic love, as well as a book on the subject, all of you are limerents.

"Limerent" is a word invented by Professor Tennov. It goes like this: A limerent is a person who falls in love. A limerent object is the one with whom a limerent is in love. And limerence describes the state of being in love, a word Tennov coined to specify that state, to distinguish it from other aspects of love, such as concern and caring. Tennov says that, just as limerent people are able to fall in love, non-limerent people are not.

Though it is often assumed that women are the limerents of this world, and men, the limerent objects, Tennov disagrees. There are reasons romantic love is associated with women, because it plays into a stereotype of women's emotionality, but it does happen to men in ways that are indistinguishable from the ways it happens to women.

But how can you tell if you are a limerent or a non-limerent? The first distinguishing factor about limerence, is the preoccupation, the not-thinking-about-anything-else. A limerent will think about everything in terms of the limerent object—how he or she will like something, what he or she will say. The limerent also feels good and bad depending on what the other person does. The limerent object controls the limerent's emotions by his or her behavior, by a phone call or no phone call. There is a tremendous dependency on the actual behavior of the other person.

Is love neurotic? Yes, that's the way limerence is, and this is why love has been called a madness down through the ages. Being limerent is a kind of insanity. Yet it doesn't mean that you're crazy. Let's describe limerence as a normal maladjustment.

According to Tennov, people in love tend to focus on little things, like "her mouth" or "the way he walks," and limerents begin to emphasize the good qualities of their limerent object. It's not that they can't see the poor qualities, but they tend not to focus on them. One subject said he could feel himself looking away when his limerent object assumed an unflattering pose. It's a certain seeking out of the positive.

But limerence doesn't begin and end here, though it may happen that way. If the limerent and the limerent object begin an immediate relationship of mutuality, their affair would be nice, but mild. What you really need for definite, crazy limerence to develop is some kind of doubt. That doubt, or the play between hopefulness and uncertainty, is what causes you to be gone.

Another limerent characteristic is an enormously strong fear of rejection. This fear often works against the limerent's own best interests. They smother their limerent object with attention instead of trying to build the love interest and mutuality slowly. Even when their heads tell them to say no, they can't.

For non-limerent individuals, this love process stops early without his or her ever being aware of anything extraordinary. They are more practical about their romantic involvements. For the limerents of this world, it's a whole different ball game.

To study love is a positive approach—and very important to learning all about it, its joys and its pains. But it's also important to study the lack of love, and narcissism is one form of this. Many people think that narcissists love themselves, but the opposite is true.

Psychology Today had a terrific article in June, 1978, by Dr. Otto Kernberg, who was interviewed by Linda Wolfe. He said that the reason why some people can't love is that they are incapable of loving themselves and they cannot give to their partners in a relationship—nor can they ever be really satisfied by what they receive. He also said that the causes of this are in childhood, and the cures are in middle age. Dr. Kernberg is a psychoanalyst, and he makes a careful distinction between normal and pathological narcissism. Some analysts see the preoccupation with self as evidence of a growing narcissism in the national character, but Dr. Kernberg says we are all in love with ourselves to some extent, and seek validation through the approval of others. He says that the pathological narcissist differs from the rest of us in the extreme intensity of his self-absorption, and suffers from a psychological ailment that requires treatment. The pathological narcissist does not really love himself at all, he actually holds himself in low esteem, and Dr. Kernberg argues that it is self-hatred and not self-love that lies at the root of pathological narcissism. We all have narcissistic tendencies and spend time and effort trying to gain the admiration and approval of others, but if our self-esteem is totally dependent on the admiration and approval of others, then something is wrong with us. He says the pathological narcissist cannot sustain his or her self-esteem without having it fed constantly by the attentions of others. Narcissists lack emotional depth and are especially lacking in genuine feelings of sadness. When abandoned or disappointed by others they appear to be depressed, but this emerges as anger rather than real sadness at the loss of a person whom they appreciated. Most of them have never been in love, says Dr. Kernberg, because the capacity to fall in love implies the ability to idealize another person, and as soon as an idealized person responds to the narcissist, the idealized person loses his or her value. Sexual fulfillment gratifies the narcissist's need for conquest and the narcissist tires of that person and moves on to the next conquest. This gives the narcissist a feeling of power (to make up for the self-loathing) but in time, dropping lovers becomes a losing proposition because the narcissist begins to understand that all liaisons will be exactly the same, no matter how sexy or attractive the partner. Dr. Kernberg says that in order to feel fulfilled we must feel deeply for others, that there is something that happens to a person in a deep relationship which brings great satisfaction, the sense of opening up and expanding beyond oneself and feeling a sense of unity with everyone who has ever lived and loved and suffered before—and when this can't be achieved, one feels emptiness and a real dissatisfaction with life.

Dr. Robert L. Spitzer, a psychiatrist, says that there are many people whose narcissism is so extreme that it becomes a disorder in its own right. We tend to think of narcissists as filled with self-love, but they are people totally without love, with such an extremely low opinion of themselves that they need the constant approval of others. Because narcissists are sick people and they make it appear that they are full of love (they're generally charming people, according to all the doctors), they cause a lot of heartaches for those unfortunate enough to be around them. I've had an experience or two and it's pathetic.

Desire is something that scares a lot of people—they seem to be afraid of their own desires. Maybe it's because they don't think their deepest desires will ever be realized, so they figure if they squash them before they get too big, nobody'll be frustrated.

In reality, desire is the bottom line to getting what you want. When you have great desire, that is the motivation to do everything. Wishing *will* make it so. But as a film director told me a few years ago, "Desire without determination is nothing." When you begin to feel the want of something, you image-in to your mind exactly what it is you want. And as the desire grows stronger, so does the mental picture. I believe when there is a positive desire (as opposed to a negative desire, or something that will hurt yourself or others), that positive desire is there because it's a part of you, part of your nature.

Desire is different from compulsion. Desire is positive and compulsion is negative. Positive desire is in relaxation and is for positive things, like becoming a teacher, artist, telephone lineman, TV director, yacht owner, etc., and compulsion is in tension and is for negative things, like gambling, over-cleaning your pad, crime, etc.

Positive desire comes from love. Negative desire comes from fear. If you desire a million dollars and figure out how to do or make something that will make the money, some job or product or idea that you love to do, that's a positive desire. If you desire the million bucks and are afraid you'll never be able to make it and you think of stealing it or bilking someone out of it or deliberately making something inferior and trying to foist it on the public, that's a negative desire. Love is positive; fear is negative.

A lumberjack may dream of owning 1,000 acres of timberland in Wyoming, but I never would. That desire comes from his psyche, the very core of his being. And he would never dream of owning a brownstone one block from Bloomies in mid-Manhattan (like me!). If you dream of being a rock star, or a cosmonaut, or president of AT & T, or a top dress designer, those desires come from your very essence and they belong to only you. No one else has exactly the same desires that you have—they may be similar, but they're different. If your desire is strong enough, you will be likely to have the determination to follow it through. And the stronger you can make the desire, the better, because that will make you even more determined.

Desire is the first step in falling in love—the desire for physical contact, for touching, the desire for emotional intimacy and spiritual unity with your beloved. But again, desire without determination is wasted. As poet Edmund Spenser said long ago— "Faint heart ne'er won fair lady." Faint heart never won *anything*.

Kahlil Gibran's *The Prophet* very sagely advises about the desires of love:

> Love has no other desire but to fulfill itself.
> But if you love and must needs have desires, let these be your desires:
> To melt and be like a running brook that sings its melody to the night.
> To know the pain of too much tenderness.
> To be wounded by your own understanding of love.
> And to bleed willingly and joyfully.
> To wake at dawn with a winged heart and give thanks for another day of loving;
> To rest at the noon hour and meditate love's ecstasy;
> To return home at eventide with gratitude;
> And then to sleep with a prayer for the beloved in your heart and a song of praise upon your lips.

Not long ago a darling friend of mine gave me a beautiful book by John Powell called *The Secret of Staying in Love.* In it, he tells the story of his father's death and how the first thing his mother said after the death was:

> "Oh, he was so proud of you. He loved you so much."

He tells how these words brought him a sharp edge of pain, as though he were going to know his father better in death than he'd ever known him while he was alive. Then, when the doctor was verifying his father's death, he was crying softly and a nurse came over to comfort him, but he couldn't talk through his tears. He says he wanted desperately to tell her:

> I'm not crying because my father is dead. I'm crying because my father never told me that he was proud of me. He never told me that he loved me. Of course I was expected to know these things. I was expected to know the great part I played in his life and the great part I occupied of his heart, but he never told me.

We *all* need to be told. I need to be told (oh, do I!), you need to be told. John Powell needs to be told, and as much as we need to be told, we need to tell. We all need to tell someone about the beautiful feelings we experience, and the more we express them, the stronger these feelings grow.

I love you. I love your dress, your hair, your slacks, your tie, your car, your apartment. But I also love *you*. I like you, too, but I also *love* you. The more you say it, the easier it becomes. But if you have any trouble at the beginning in saying it, you can always say "Isle of view." Nobody'll ever know the difference, and think how terrific it'll be when we're all saying it.

Isle of view.

ISLE OF VIEW

7

How To Be A Great Lover

USE AMERICA'S ARMS FOR HUGGING
—Illinois Police Federation

On one of my many visits to Chicago to do TV shows, I was in a cab going from the airport to the hotel when I saw that sign, which is probably the most terrific sign I've ever seen. It was very big and attached to the side of a building about halfway into the city. Whoever thought of that sign—now there's a lover—a person who knows love and is full of it. Just imagine: no more guns, just lots of hugging. That really turned me on.

What does it mean to be a great lover? It means one who is capable of loving. Why is it that whenever we hear the word "lover," we usually think of sex? To be a great lover means far more than being proficient at sex. Anyone can buy a sex manual (there sure are hundreds of them around) and memorize the different positions and make mental notes of the drawings or photographs and practice for the next six years and *still* not be a great lover. After all, we don't say making sex, we say making love, so sex and positions and body parts are only a small area regarding love. Sex is the "after the fact," which is the icing on the cake after you've become loving.

A lover is one who loves, or cares for something or someone. To be a truly great lover one must love many things—music, art, beauty, animals, people. I don't believe it's possible to hate, or not care for, music, art, beauty and most people and then be a great lover of one man or woman. Love is all-encompassing. If I have the capacity to deeply love music and appreciate it, if I am able to love great art and visit the Metropolitan Museum of Art or the Louvre and truly appreciate Rodin or Michelangelo or Monet, if I care for animals and am distressed if one is lost or in pain and I try to help it, if I see that someone is emotionally suffering and I try to say something to alleviate the pain—then I am capable of truly caring for one other human being and loving him or her.

Many of us are all blocked off emotionally and keep our feelings guarded so they don't dare escape. We feel embarrassed to let someone see us cry in a sad movie—we don't want anyone to know how deeply we are moved. It embarrasses us to have someone see how vulnerable we are. But that very vulnerability is the basis of love.

I remember my head used to hurt in a sad movie because I was working so hard to keep from crying. I thought crying would show everyone how weak I was, and I sure didn't want anyone to see *that*. So I worked and worked to try to stifle my emotions if something made me sad when there were other people around (I never had trouble crying when I was alone). So I decided to work on releasing my emotions. I'll never forget sitting in a restaurant in Hollywood with a date I'd seen a few times and the conversation turned to something which upset me and made me sad, the death of someone we both knew. That lucky fellow was the first to watch me cry, but I must have really shook the poor thing up, because I never saw him again. You'd think maybe that would have scared me into retreating into my holding-back self, but I figured that if he didn't like the *real* me, the sometimes laughing, sometimes crying person, then he was too uptight for me and obviously the wrong person for an intimate relationship.

Nathaniel Hawthorne said about happiness, and when you read his quote, substitute "romance" for "happiness":

> Happiness in this world, when it comes, comes incidentally. Make it the object of pursuit, and it leads us on a wild goose chase and is never attained. Follow some other object, and very possibly we may find that we have caught happiness without dreaming of it; but likely enough it is gone the moment we say to ourselves, "Here it is!"

Whenever we go out searching for romance, it eludes us. I've seen too many people, desperate for love, looking all over for that certain someone, and they never find him or her. People can sense desperation and it scares them. We want to love someone who doesn't desperately need us, someone who is self-sufficient and self-reliant. Loneliness makes some people too obvious in their need for companionship, and it's pathetic because this drives any possibilities for love away. We seem to find love when we least expect it and when we're not consciously looking for it.

And once you begin a relationship, don't throw yourself totally into it until you are sure you and your partner honestly have enough in common so that there's a chance it can last. I'm beginning to think that having a lot in common (common interests, common desires) is the most important ingredient for a happy relationship—because then you can dream together, plan together and love together and have lots to talk about while you're having fun.

Is Woody Allen a great lover? I don't know, but the way he pokes fun and doesn't seem to take sex as seriously as so many people do, is a step in the right direction. Who can forget the great scene in *Bananas* when the little schnook walks up to the crowded magazine stand and leafs through several "high class" magazines, like *National Geographic*, *Business Week*, and the *New Yorker*, and picks them up; then he walks over to *Good Housekeeping*, picks it up with a *McCall's* and a *Psychology Today*. Then he sidles over to *Orgasm* magazine, surreptitiously slides it in the middle of all the other periodicals, and walks up to the cashier. She rings them all up, then holds out the one magazine and yells loudly to a guy in the back, "Hey Irving, how much is this *Orgasm?*", while our schnook dies a little as every head turns to look at him, now a flaming beet red.

Or that great scene Woody wrote and acted in *Play It Again, Sam:*

Allen: We mustn't. It's forbidden.

Linda: But these things happen. Nobody plans them.

Allen: Yes, but you're not free.

Linda: In my heart I'm free. I can't repress it any longer. At first I thought you were just a helpless, mixed-up child, but I didn't really know you then. Now I believe you're everything I ever dreamed of loving.

Allen: You poor thing. How you must've suffered —wanting me so.

Linda: My darling. I need you. I need to possess your body and soul.

Allen: Which would you like to begin with? . . .

I think having a sense of humor is one of the most important things one needs to be a great lover, and Woody sure qualifies there.

Dr. Rolland S. Parker, a psychotherapist, has written a marvelous book, *Emotional Common Sense,* which is subtitled "How to Avoid Self-Destructiveness." Rolland and I met in Baltimore a couple of years ago when both of us appeared on a TV show and talked about our books. We rode the Metroliner back to New York together and got to know a little about each other during the ninety-minute ride. I was very impressed with him and with his book, which I read later that day. Then we lost contact until a few months ago, when we bumped into each other at a Mensa meeting. When I got home I looked for his book, took it out and reread it. He talks about self-destructiveness, sexual self-destructiveness, overcoming loneliness and deprivation and achieving meaningful sexual relationships. One of his chapters defines a good lover:

> Being a good lover requires enthusiasm; it implies pleasing the partner. But it also requires a receptive attitude. It means that you expect and are willing to experience pleasure.
>
> I think a good lover is knowledgeable and open-minded. Some reasonable balance is required between technique and the spiritual qualities of the relationship. There are plenty of sexual manuals available which can give you guides to variety and other ways of enhancing sexuality.
>
> I think that a positive attitude toward sex and one's partner during the experience is also essential. To bring into the bedroom one's needs to be dependent, to express hostility, to dominate, to reject, and so forth, is an invitation to frustration. These unresolved problems lead to such disorders as premature ejaculation or potency problems in the man and frigidity or refusal to have sex in the woman. Leave your problems outside the bedroom.
>
> What about the question of commitment? This can't

be answered without reference to the decision to engage in exclusive or multiple relationships. If one or both partners are committed to the one-night stand, then being a good lover simply means having good technique, being sensitive to the wishes and feelings of the other, having the capacity to respond within the limits required by the other person, and similar technical considerations. But if one person will not have sexuality without knowing that there is a firm relationship, then frustration and retreat are likely to occur. For some, the opposite frame of mind holds: they do not wish to have a sense of obligation. Honest people will express their attitudes before they get undressed.

Then there's consideration. There are so many external circumstances which affect a person's sexuality. It is true that a larger proportion of men seem more sexually eager than women, but this is up to the point of encounter. Then the roles may become reversed or equalized. However, when a couple live together and do not have to engage in courtship rituals, they must have consideration for each other to a greater extent.

I think that expressiveness is also part of being a good lover. Let your partner know what you feel, what you enjoy, even what you don't like or want changed. Since your enjoyment is vital to both of you, assuming that the relationship is really viable, you cannot ignore any possibility of letting your partner know how he can please you, provided you are willing to be pleased! If you are pleased, say so, encourage more sex, let the good spirits affect all parts of your relationship.

Finally, part of being a good lover is not being obnoxious.

Not being obnoxious—don't you love it? After Dr. Parker lists all those terrific qualifications, he ends with not being obnoxious. You can be enthusiastic, and knowledgeable and open-minded, and have a positive attitude toward sex and have consideration, and still be a pain in the neck, which, of course, is not a thrilling turn-on.

To me, kindness is the biggest turn-on of all. I remember a few years ago I was walking down Fifth Avenue in front of the Sherry-Netherlands Hotel and I saw a German shepherd running loose on the sidewalk. This is very unusual in New York because of the stringent leash law. At the same time I saw the dog, a young man saw him, too. Before I had a chance to try to catch the dog, the man had taken his tie off and was chasing the dog, which he finally (after about ten minutes) caught. The dog surely would have been killed by traffic (as all New Yorkers know, there are lots of cars here). This man ruined his tie, spent a lot of time and energy, risked his own life by stopping traffic as the dog ran in and out of the street, and then found a cop who called the ASPCA to come fetch the dog. But that man was a lover.

Another time I was on my way to the airport when the cab hit a terrific jam-up on the FDR Drive. I thought I'd miss my plane, so I got out of the cab to see what was holding us up, and about ten cars ahead there were three men who had stopped traffic going both ways because there was a little frightened dog who had wandered out on the highway and would have gotten killed in a second if it hadn't been for the kindness of these men. Cars were honking, people were cursing, but these guys went along unfazed till they caught the poor little thing and saved his life. I was so impressed and touched (I always am by kindness) that I wrote my first and last "letter to the editor" of the New York *Times* (which they didn't print). I didn't care—I just wanted to show that the sometime image drawn of New Yorkers being cold and impersonal is certainly not true. When people go out of their way to help another person or an animal, that's beautiful. That's what being a great lover is all about. Not only having the enormous capacity to love, but expressing it in many ways.

There is a wonderful book I found called *Love* written by Leo Buscaglia. In it he tells about how he started an experimental course at USC called "Love Class," how successful it was, and how his book on love was an outgrowth of this "Love Class." His basic theory is that love is learned, and that everyone can and should learn to love and to be a lover. Some of his notes from his "Love Class" are:

One does not fall in or out of love. One grows in love.

Real love always creates. It never destroys.

Love goes beyond hope. Hope is a beginning. Love is forever.

Man has no choice but to love. For when he does not, he finds his alternatives lie in loneliness, destruction and despair.

When man has love, he is no longer at the mercy of forces greater than himself, for he himself becomes the powerful force.

When you love yourself, you will love others. And to the depth and extent to which you can love yourself, only to that depth and extent will you be able to love others.

Love and the self are one, and the desiring of either is the realization of both.

If one wishes to be a lover, he must start by saying yes to love.

Another wonderful book was written by Jo Coudert, called *Advice From A Failure,* in which she says that if you treat everyone well, love will follow:

It is one of those quirks of human nature that you love the person whom you treat well, not necessarily the person who treats you well. Love follows the trail blazed by generosity. Lincoln once said something to the effect that if he wanted a person to like him, he asked him to do him a favor; that is, he asked him to lend him a book rather than offering to lend the other a book. So it is in marriage: instead of coming to despise the other for his faults, if you behave with tact and understanding and good will, your love will increase. You will become ever more fond of the person you behave excellently toward. Thus, although it would seem at first glance that forbearance and patience and silence might exact almost too heavy a toll to bear, the opposite is true. The other will benefit, but it is you who will benefit greatly, for you will love more—more, perhaps than you thought possible, and that is an incomparable feeling. We all know we want to be loved, and we speak of this, but we are less aware of just how much we wish to love. We want somebody in whom we can put the immense amount of love we sense we have. We want somebody who is worth all that love. What we do not realize is that we can *create* somebody who is worth all that love by loving him well.

Then she says:

It is not necessary to love so that we may give. It is necessary to give so that we may love.

I've read a great deal about the "will to live" and I've found the premise is true. Where there is a strong will to live it counteracts many negative forces. A man can be dying and the doctors may have given up all hope, yet the man lives. The doctors usually explain it by saying he had a strong will to live. Or a woman is poised on the ledge of a thirty-second-floor window of a midtown hotel and threatens to jump. The police are mobilized to try to dissuade her from leaping. The newspapers are out en masse to record her trauma. Finally, after ten hours of indecision, they coax her back into the room. Her will to live was stronger than her emotional upheaval or her death-wish. So living is something we all will, consciously or unconsciously. Yet some people do choose to die, either through out-and-out suicide or the slow way—too many pills and drugs, or the very slow way—too much booze and cigarettes (drugs, but they're legal). I believe that people who drink or smoke heavily have a definite death-wish, and those who stop drinking and smoking obviously have a stronger will to live. So our wills are important to living. Either we choose to or not.

We also have a will to love—and a will not to love. When you see a person holding back love and terrified of expressing it, he or she has willed, consciously or unconsciously, not to love. Just as the will to live can be strengthened by various methods (analysis, therapy, self-hypnosis), the same thing can happen with the will to love. The most important step is to recognize that the will to not love exists—then you can either live with that fact or try to do something to change it. The will to not love *always* stems from fear. Something happened in the past that so frightened the person that he or she is unable to function as a loving human being. The saddest part about people not able to express love is that not only are they estranged from the joy of affection and pleasure, but those around them have to suffer too. How many spouses are hungering for a show of love from their partners, only to be rebuffed by a cold reception? And how many children have to grow up around a cold, distant parent when the kids would give anything for a bear hug and the security that an "Isle of View" gives?

Wouldn't it be terrific if we were all able to hug and kiss freely and say I love you? Little kids, older people, teenagers—it's not such an impossible dream. Once we all start feeling sensational physically, mentally and emotionally, so that we're able to really cope with all our so-called problems, we can start spreading some hugs and kisses to the little kids in the world, because that's where it all begins. A few months ago I was behind an old beat-up station wagon and saw its bumper sticker: "HAVE YOU HUGGED YOUR KID TODAY?"

We all respond to love, be it a hug, a kiss or an I love you, but children especially soak up warmth and affection like sponges. Several years ago I spotted a poster I never forgot:

CHILDREN LEARN WHAT
THEY LIVE WITH

> If a child lives with criticism,
>   he learns to condemn;
> If a child lives with hostility,
>   he learns to fight;
> If a child lives with ridicule,
>   he learns to be shy;
> If a child lives with shame,
>   he learns to feel guilty;
> If a child lives with tolerance,
>   he learns to be patient;
> If a child lives with encouragement,
>   he learns confidence;
> If a child lives with praise,
>   he learns to appreciate;
> If a child lives with fairness,
>   he learns justice;
> If a child lives with security,
>   he learns to have faith;

If a child lives with approval,
   he learns to like himself;
If a child lives with acceptance and
friendship,
   he learns how to find love in the
world.

I know that when I was a kid I was given an enormous amount of love (squeezed between hostility and anger and fear, which were also given to me), and because of this I always wanted to express love. When I was eight years old I used to walk down the street and say hello to strangers. They all smiled and said hello back. One day my aunt saw me doing this and told me I shouldn't (maybe she was right, but isn't it a shame we can't do this all our lives instead of being suspicious and full of fear?). Then, when I was a teenager, I got my first car, and one night it was pouring rain and I saw a man hitchhiking and I stopped to pick him up. I'll never forget the man, drenched and dripping water all over the front seat of my car lecturing me about why I should never pick up a stranger. I guess I've always been looking for the utopia of everyone loving everyone else, and unless we all start, it'll never happen. People say to me, "Yeah, but what about all the crime and murders? You can't trust everybody."

I have my own philosophy. I don't believe there's any good or any evil. I believe there just *is*. It's a chair, not a good chair or a bad chair, just a chair. It may be a blue chair, which is a fact, but it's not good or bad, which are value-judgments. Things that are "good" are things which please me. "Bad" things are things that displease me. I am a tall, red-haired person, not good and not evil, I just am. Adjectives are okay to describe something like green or tall or wide or heavy. But certain words are only opinions, like comfortable (a chair may be comfortable to a 5'8" person like me and very uncomfortable to a 4'8" person like you) or easy (it may be an easy test for a brilliant person like you and more difficult for a less brilliant person like me) or good (it may have been a good talk for you but it bored me to tears) or bad (you thought the movie was awful but I really loved it). Good and bad and hard and easy are judgments we make. A "good" person does things that I like and a "bad" person does things that I don't like. But he or she is still just a person, not good or bad. Someone recently stole my wallet out of my purse and I was very bugged. All my money and all my credit cards and personal items were gone. I was very angry that this "bad" person robbed me. I spent a lot of time with the police and stopping all my credit cards and looking in neighborhood trash cans for the wallet and personal things. I was tense and upset, so I lay down on my slant-board and thought about it. The person who robbed me was just a person—a screwed-up person, a confused person, but not "bad." He (I found out it was a he) thought the only way to make money was to steal and that's very sad. All the energy he put into robbing people could have been used constructively to make money for him in another area which could have given him pride in himself. My upsetness dissipated and I visualized getting my wallet back, then I did my mental exercise: "God

adores me and wants me to have my wallet back."
I didn't care as much about the money; I wanted my
personal things. Three days later the rector of a
nearby church called me and said he found my wallet in the gutter, and when I got it everything but
the money was intact. The rector isn't a "good" man
(although he brought me happiness) and the thief
isn't a "bad" man (although he brought me unhappiness)—they're just men doing what they think is
making them happy. The thief may be a confused or
emotionally disturbed man, but because he dis-
pleases me doesn't make him "bad." "Bad" is an
emotive word that makes me angry and I don't like
to be angry because angry upsets me emotionally
and makes me tense. "Confused" or "emotionally
disturbed" makes me intellectually try to figure out
how to handle the situation, what to do to uncon-
fuse the thief or emotionally disturbed person. Do
we put the thief in jail and for how long? Do we
change his physical diet with vites and minerals and
his mental diet with a psychiatrist or analyst? Can
we use people in prison in some way to better society (make shoes for orphans, paint public buildings)? Is it possible this person can be un-confused
and emotionally straightened out and return to society a changed person ready to work with us instead
of against us? If we look at him, without anger, as
just a person—we can be objective and dispassionate
and maybe even compassionate, but with anger, and
looking at him as a "bad" person it's difficult to see
things as clearly. The end result, however, might be
the same. Locking him up so he can't rob others
seems to be the best we've come up with yet, until

he can learn to respect himself and his own property (even if his only property is his body) and then other people's property.

Everyone is different, not better or worse, just different. Some basic things about us are the same (we're all born, we all feel pain, we all are capable of joy and laughter, we all die), but we're also all very very different (you like to paint, he likes to play softball, I like to write music). So we realize that we're all here not because we asked to be but because we were just born, we might also realize that we're all looking for happiness in our different ways. What makes you happy doesn't necessarily work for me and vice versa. I'm a total fatalist—I believe we must do everything we can (without hurting our selves or others) to try to attain our goals and then we must relax and know that the end result is going to happen the way it should. Lots of people think that fatalism is just staying in bed all day because "what will be will be," but that's not fatalism, that's just dopeyness. True fatalism is knowing there's a master plan, going out and doing your thing, and knowing that *after you've done all you can,* "what will be, will be." This gets rid of mental anxiety, or worrying something to death before it happens, and it also gets rid of regret, or wishing you hadn't done something after it happens. Things happen because they are supposed to happen, they were meant to happen, and even though it may not appear to be to your liking, or to be the right thing, it always is. Maybe the pain it brought is there for you to learn from, to actively make some changes in your life and get out of your mental or emotional rut. I used to worry about most everything before it happened and I used to regret most everything after it happened. But the more I thought about it, the dumber it seemed and the more logical fatalism was. If I believed in God (or Love or Giant Self or Spirit), and that God is Love and Love is God, and I am the object of this Love, then:

1. Why am I worrying that something will go wrong before it happens?
2. Why am I worrying that something did go wrong and I'm wishing I could do it over, constantly berating myself that if I hadn't done such and such, then this would never have happened and if I had only not said what I said, then none of the awful things would have happened?
3. Why am I worrying about *anything?*

I just do my thing and know that what is meant to be will be. I am in my right place *now*—if it weren't right, I wouldn't be here, I'd be someplace else.

And these feelings that God is Love and Love is God help make me a bigger and better lover.

Frank Gifford says that great sex is part of being a great lover, but certainly not all—there's *no* great sex without real love, and *total* satisfaction comes with the one you really love. He says, "Sex, when it's right, gets better with time as you get to know each other. People probably have other problems when sex lessens after years." Frank believes that the *only* really rewarding thing in life (and he says he *really* believes this) is love, and that he shows lots of love to his wife and kids and dog, and that it never embarrasses him. He says that the men who are blocked off and afraid of emotional commitment are generally super-macho men who have hangups about their own masculinity. Men who are fairly sure of themselves can be gentle and warm and loving. Frank feels that love is learned and grows stronger from associating with people who do care for us. He says his mother and father were married fifty-three or fifty-four years (he can't remember which), and they were really in love all the way. Frank says when he talks to his kids on the phone, he *never* hangs up without saying "I love you."

Jane Fonda, who won an Oscar for *Klute* and an Oscar nomination for *Julia*, considers herself a survivor, and she's survived a lot. Because she's a woman full of love and conscience, she became a passionate antiwar activist, and that almost wrecked her career, but she didn't care. Because she's an uncompromising person and she felt the war was immoral, she did everything in her power to call attention to that fact. She married a political activist, Tom Hayden (no relation to me, except we're both Irish), and now the two of them are working together politically to make some major changes within the system. Jane is a very courageous woman with the guts to put her money, career and life where her mouth is. She's strong and intense, and yet a warm and loving person who cares about humanity. Her love comes out in her activism. I don't agree with all of her political views, but if true religion is love in action, then Jane Fonda is expressing God in every part of her life.

To be a great lover you must not only love a great many things and people, but you must also be loved by most people. You can't be a loving person and have lots of people dislike you or hate you. And that brings up something that I feel is awfully important to being a great lover and bringing love and happiness to everyone around you. I believe in "creative lying." Now all lying is creative in the sense that a person is making something up from his or her imagination, but lying is generally negative and is based on fear. My "creative lying" is positive and based on caring for people, like telling "white lies" to make people feel good. To do "creative lying" you must truly love people and also have an active imagination. Now I don't mean this in the sense of making up and telling untruths, I mean creating fantasies which could actually happen or become possibilities of things that could actually happen, and which make people happy and give them hope. We all need hope, and the luckier ones of us have lots of it. We're lucky because our mothers or fathers or teachers or *somebody* led us to believe in the possibilities of life. *Anything* is possible to the person who hopes and dreams and images-in all the terrific things in life that are fun.

So to do "creative lying" you *never* tell anyone anything that will discourage (dis-courage or un-courage) him or her, even though it seems apparent that there is no hope for that person to do or be or make something. "Creative lying" finds something positive (and there's always *something* positive in everything) and embroiders that, and imaginatively leads the person to believe that he or she can do or be or make something. If you love your self (and all lovers start first with loving themselves), then you won't ever discourage yourself—you'll figure out how to do or be or make something, and once you learn to do this for your self, it becomes much easier to do for others. For instance, I never berate my self anymore. I used to do it a lot, but when I figured out how dumb it was, and how badly it made me feel, I stopped. Now, when I do something I'm not proud of, I realize that at the moment I did it I *had* to do it (I had several options at the moment, and I weighed each one and chose what to me *at that moment* seemed the wisest and best thing to do, and had I been able to do something else, I would have), and I try to learn from that experience. Well, it's the same with friends or lovers. He or she may not be proud of what happened, but berating can only make it worse, while "creative lying," or blocking out the negative and focusing on the positive and using your imagination to help the situation, is beautiful.

I'll give you two examples—I do lots of guest appearances on TV shows and sometimes I do a terrific job and sometimes I don't. A lot depends on the interviewer—some TV hosts are great and some aren't. Once I did a show and I was just awful. The woman interviewing me was a lox and there was another woman guest who didn't like me a bit (and we'd never met before so I don't know what her problem was), and the guest was ripping me apart and the host didn't know how to handle the situation, so every time I'd open my mouth the other guest would interrupt me very rudely—oh, it was a shambles. It was taped, so several days later I watched it with a friend. Now I knew it was awful, I knew more than anybody how awful it was, so I sure didn't need his criticism (I only watched it to see if I could figure out if there had been something I could have done to have saved myself from the massacre). I knew every little thing that was wrong (I think each person is probably much more critical of his or her own work than anybody else could ever be). Well, he started criticizing me and it was a blitzkrieg. I silently wrote him off and I told him that I knew it was awful so I didn't need his negatives, but on he went. It was a disastrous evening and I lost a friend (?).

The second example was a rerun of a TV guest-star appearance I had made with a well-known male star. The director of the show should have either been driving a cab, sweeping the street, or selling hot dogs on the corner of Fifty-eighth Street and Fifth Avenue, but he sure shouldn't have been directing our show. It was awful, and we all knew it. I was with another friend when I watched it, but my friend was adorable. He knew I didn't do a good job, but he told me I did. It's funny how, when we want to believe something, we will, and I started to believe it wasn't really so bad. He loved certain things (which I hadn't even seen, I was so unhappy over the show), the way I wore my hair and the way I did certain lines. He was sensational. By the end of the show I really believed it wasn't so awful and I started to feel better. He was using "creative lying" to make me happy and it worked (I once heard two people discussing a third—one said that the guy was really nasty inside and covered it up with niceness and charm on the outside, and the other said that that was okay with him; as long as the person kept his awfulness inside and acted nice to everyone, it was a pleasure). So the TV show I did was awful. There was nothing I could do to change that, and I'd much rather feel good than feel terrible, so my friend was really my friend, and he truly cared for me, not wanting to see me feeling awful but wanting to make me feel okay.

Like an actor (I don't remember who) once said to someone criticizing his work, "I don't want you to criticize me, I want you to love me." And that's the truth. Who needs a knocker? Now that's not to say we can't use constructive criticism, but that's what "creative lying" is. It's finding the good, and helping change the not-so-good in a constructive (not destructive) way. The man who made me feel good about my performance is truly my friend. I love him 'cause he loves me. I love people who love me (doesn't everybody?). So to be a great lover, be loving with everyone and everything—water your plants, wash your face, apologize to someone even though you think you were right, say hello to the mailman and give him a big smile, make everybody feel as good as you do.

CHAPTER 8

Pleasuring You

ONE OF THE most thrilling, exciting and satisfying things about being in love is pleasuring the person you're crazy about. From buying a Rolls Royce and handing the keys to your beloved (wouldn't you faint?), to sending a funny little card or a pair of socks (because you noticed a hole in the toe of his) or a single flower. That's part of the romance of love, and life without romance is a bore.

They say that romance is making a big comeback, but I'm not sure it ever left. There are always those romantic souls who love to do romantic things and there have always been non-romantics, who think romance is a waste of time. People will always send flowers, dance slow dances, and ask for movies about love rather than sex. Touch-dancing will always be popular and when you go to the discos you will always see some people asking for the slower,

more romantic songs and you will notice some people hugging on the dance floor. What a turn-on
when you're with someone you dig! Holding hands,
hugging, touching—the signs of affection are all
around us and will always be with us, no matter
what else is in vogue. If you saw *Barbarella*, the
futuristic Roger Vadim film starring Jane Fonda,
you'll remember the "sex scene" where a man
(David Hemmings, I believe), strapped himself to a
machine, turned it on, and the machine gave him a
sexual climax. If that's the future, what a bore! If I
want to pleasure you, I sure don't want to strap you
into a chair, turn on a machine, and watch you have
fun. Half the pleasure is knowing I'm able to give
you pleasure and the other half is sharing it with
you. Just knowing that you care for me turns me on
so that I can't wait to do terrific things to pleasure
you and make you happy.

Dr. Wardell B. Pomeroy, a researcher and therapist, believes that sex with love is much more important than great sexual techniques without love, and
he says that in the past, sex was usually considered
an expression of romantic love, but now the empha-
sis is on sexual techniques and variety of sexual acts
that gives many people the impression that this is all
they need for sexual pleasure. He says that love is
not extraneous to sexual pleasure, and he believes
that the idea that techniques are all-important is a
new myth—that sexual techniques are certainly
helpful, but that it's the quality of the interpersonal
relationship that's going to determine the quality of
the sex, not the techniques. Dr. Pomeroy definitely
believes that we need to get more fun into sex, but

that there can also be solemn or serious or quiet moments, and that basically sex can encompass a complete range—from animal-like abandon to thoughtful interchange, and that for some, sex represents a profound bond and for others (or even the same people at different times), it is a recreational experience.

Sex is reality—a physical fact—but love is romance, fantasy, dreams, and dreams are the motivating factor in life. One of my all-time favorite poems (I don't know the author), which I memorized when I was a kid and I think about often, goes:

> Remember this when the dark days
>   fall,
> That the compass and caliper lie.
> Your life is great or your life is small,
> By your dreams that live or die.

So if I give you sex, that's all well and good and basic, but sex is something everyone has and can give and get. We all possess bodies—some shorter, some taller, some thinner, some fatter. We have breasts and sexual organs in all different sizes and shapes. We have lips and tongues and hands and fingers, so just to have sex is no great accomplishment. But to have sex with love . . . that's the dream.

As Mae West said, sex is great, but sex with love can drive you mad!

I want to give you more. I want to pleasure you with loving and caring and affection. I want to light the fire of your imagination so we can dream together. I want to soar with you to all the places we both could go. I want to fantasize with you and paint dreams of things neither one of us ever knew existed. I want to romance you and have you romance me—do all the things we know will make us happy and give us pleasure.

I want to do all of this through my love for you. I want to make you believe that you can do things you never thought possible. I want to build up your ego so that you will believe you are the greatest person in the world. If I can make you believe this it will free you from self-doubt and fear, and will open you up so we can share everything together. Lots of people are afraid that if their lover's ego is strong, the lover will no longer need them, but that's wrong. Only a person who believes in himself, and loves himself for being a good and strong person, can truly love another person.

And it must be mutual. You must really care for *each other*. Unfortunately, lots of love affairs are one-sided, but when they are, they're doomed. Love is a constantly changing, ever-growing feeling, and the warmth and affection of your partner for you encourages your love to grow. And as your love grows, the warmth and affection from it encourages your partner's love, and on it goes. If you offer warmth and affection and it's rejected, you can pretend it doesn't bother you, and you can continue being with your partner and taking care of him or her, but the real feeling of love, that wonderful deep feeling that life *is* a bowl of cherries and you're savoring each juicy, shiny red one, that feeling will leave (if it was there at the beginning), or will never begin. It's the same as an actor reacting to an audience.

When the audience loves your performance or the play, and sends waves of love and applause over the footlights, the actor opens up and gives one hundred and ten percent of his or her self. But if the audience doesn't like the play or the performance, and rejects you with little or no applause, you sense the coldness, tighten up and give ten percent of what you could. It's all reaction. Warmth begets warmth—and chills beget chills.

Even in a crowd of people, you can sense who likes you and who doesn't. The person whom you feel really likes you or who is attracted to you, that's the person you generally feel better around and want to get to know better. Love attracts—fear rejects.

Milton Mayeroff is a noted philosopher who feels that if man can ever be said to be at home in the world it will be not through dominating, or explaining, or appreciating, but through caring and being cared for. In his book *On Caring* he says:

> In caring for another person I encourage him, I inspire him to have the courage to be himself. My trust in him encourages him to trust himself and to be worthy of the trust. Perhaps few things are more encouraging to another than to realize that his growth evokes admiration, a spontaneous delight or joy, in the one who cares for him. He experiences my admiration as assuring him that he is not alone and that I am really for him. . . . The man who is not needed by someone or something does not belong and lives like a leaf blown about in the wind. I have a need to be needed

and the need of others for me goes hand in hand with my need for them.

He goes on to say:

In a meaningful friendship, caring is mutual, each cares for the other; caring becomes contageous. My caring for the other helps activate his caring for me; and similarly his caring for me helps activate my caring for him, it "strengthens" me to care for him.

So the greatest pleasuring you can do is to make your spouse or roomie or friend feel loved and appreciated by you. Because when a person knows and feels valued by someone he or she values, the feeling of self-worth grows immensely and that person begins to like him or her self, and to open up emotionally and give back to you the love and appreciation.

Dr. Frederick Humphrey, past president of the American Association of Marriage and Family Counselors, believes you must keep romance alive in your relationships, and if you are married, treat your spouse just exactly as if he or she were your lover, and put the same kind of energy and imagination into your marriage as you would into an extramarital affair. No one's going to argue with that. Who wants to be taken for granted? Not me. I want to feel my husby or boyfriend thinks of me as somebody special. After all, isn't that what we're all striving for, to be special, whether it's through our jobs or our hobbies or our relationships with people? Nobody wants to be a blob and feel the world wouldn't miss him or her a second.

Frances Wilshire wrote a wonderful little book called *You*, in which she talks about the three vital laws—The Law of Attraction, The Law of Freedom and The Law of Balance.

First, The Law of Attraction:

> If you wish to make anything attractive to yourself or to others, you make it so romantic, interesting, beautiful and intriguing that its own attractiveness is its power to attract. In this way you touch or arouse the feeling, or emotional, nature. Whenever you succeed in arousing the emotions, you have made an impression which is not soon forgotten. People do not remember you by any intellectual idea or concept you may have given them, but by some subtle emotional impression you may have made consciously or unconsciously. It is what one thinks about you after you have left that counts.

Second, The Law of Freedom:

> The use of this law will, in itself, cause you to be a Magnet of Attraction. When a person is won by The Law of Attraction, he has come into your life of his own free will and will stay through that same power of attraction. That gives him a sense of freedom. Freedom is life. The urge of every living soul is toward freedom. What you give up, you get! By giving anything its freedom, you win it! When you free any limiting thoughts or feelings, then their binding power or influence is gone, and you sense a freedom you never knew before.

Third, the Law of Balance:

> Your balance is found by what we call The Law of
> Spiritual Equilibrium, which means half to yourself
> and half to the world. The first half, which is to give
> to yourself, is so essential that without it the second
> half becomes impossible of attainment. You must first
> give your entire attention to the improvement, the
> knowledge, and the development of yourself. You
> must spend your time, your effort, and your money,
> first on yourself. For you must first have strength,
> vitality, wisdom, or money, to be able to give and
> thereby to fulfill the second half, which in other words
> is service. You cannot give unless you have something
> to give.

So before you can pleasure anyone else, you must
pleasure yourself. Assuming that you're getting
your body in great shape with the Dynamite Milkshake and vites and you're doing your exercises
every day, and you've found the job you really
groove in or you're planning to take an aptitude test
so that you *will* find your life's work, NOW is the
time to start thinking about pleasuring others. If
you're not ready yet, don't rush it. Wait till you start
to feel pretty good about yourself—then you can
start to feel pretty good about others.

It's *fun* to do little things for others because people are usually so surprised and grateful that it
makes you feel terrific. For instance, when you walk
into or out of a room through a swinging door, just
glance back to see if anyone is behind you, and if so,
hold the door till the person gets there (instead of

letting the door slam into them). The appreciation is usually surprising. And it makes you feel good to know you've made someone else feel good. You can actually make sort of a game out of it (and God knows we could use a little more fun in life, right?). Think of coocoo ways to pleasure the world at large. I remember a couple of years ago I was walking down Third Avenue near my apartment and I saw a policeman approaching a car in front of an expired meter, so I walked over and put a dime in and the cop walked away, thinking it was my car. I got halfway down the street when I heard a guy yelling, "Miss, miss!" so I stopped and it was the car's owner. He had been in a men's store shopping and had seen me put the dime in and the cop walk away. Now I did it just for my own kicks, pleasuring myself about saving somebody from getting a ticket, but because he saw me and chased after me, I made a new friend. He asked me why I did it and I told him for fun (which at first he found hard to believe), but I told him if he didn't believe it was fun, to try it himself the next time he saw a car with a run-out parking meter. It really makes you feel good when you do something nice. Sometime when you see an old person, try holding the door open for him or her, and you won't believe the gratefulness expressed. And it really makes you feel terrific.

I've tried analyzing why this makes me feel so good and I've come up with my own answer. When I do something nice (like holding open a door for someone) and the person is really surprised and happy and grateful, they become aware of love and good in this world and they might start believing that people are nice and good and kind, and that will make them happy, and then they'll start being kind and doing nice things for other people and one of the other people is me. I like doing nice things because I know in life we get what we give.

So you don't think I'm a Goody Two-Shoes, I'm not *always* good and kind to everybody. I have my moments too, when I don't feel like holding a door open or carrying an old lady's heavy bag. Sometimes I feel frustrated and/or worried about something, but I've got my mind trained not to think of negatives, so without too much effort I sweep the screen and project positive thoughts to myself. And of course my body is in truly *great* shape, because not one day goes by that I don't drink my morning milkshake and take my vites (which make my body feel sensational), and every day (even when I don't want to) I discipline myself to do all my exercises (a fast ten minutes, tops).

But I don't do things to pleasure people just because it's good or nice. I do them because they're truly fun and they make me feel good. Just stimulating your mind to come up with new and original ideas to make people feel terrific will make you feel terrific. When you see someone do something nice for someone else, it might appear that the do-er is very selfless and you might get the idea the person is trying to be saintlike, and oh, so good, but that ain't necessarily so. People who do kind things often really *enjoy* being nice—they get their kicks making other people happy. It's self-gratification, and if you don't believe it, try it.

Now, obviously, a physically sick person can't do

much for others if he or she is in physical pain or too weak to move. Physical sickness makes us very selfish—it forces a person to think only of him- or herself. Just remember when you were ill and in pain. All you could think about was your pain and how to get rid of it. By its very nature, physical illness makes us introverted and think only of ourselves. Well, the same thing happens when we're emotionally sick, or upset, or overwhelmed with problems we think we can't handle. Emotional problems make us as selfish as physical ones. That's the reason most people don't seem to care for others —they're so wrapped up in their own problems that it's impossible to think of anyone else. So, in order to help others, we must help ourselves first.

If you have physical problems, go to a doctor to see if they're serious or not. And then, on your own, change the way of life that is obviously bringing on the problems. Cut out the junk and put in the Dynamite Milkshake and vitamins, and when you start to feel super-good, start doing a few exercises to get your circulation moving. And the better you feel, the more you'll want to do. It's a growing circle. And then, as you start to feel terrific and more energetic, you'll find you're much less tense and anxious, and your depressions will go away and you'll start to feel "up" most of the time. But you still might have a few emotional problems to sort out, and if so, try talking them over with a trusted friend, or someone you don't know, like a psychologist or a marriage counselor or an analyst.

We all need help, and the biggest step is recognizing that there might be someone who could help us.

The more emotionally sick a person is, usually the less likely is that person to recognize the problem. This is generally because the problem is deep and serious and the person is petrified to let out the snakes and bats and ugliness that he or she thinks are lurking inside them. I know that when I was a kid I wouldn't acknowledge that there was anything wrong because there was so much wrong. Finally I got to the point that I realized that if I didn't get help, all the snakes and bats were going to run my life (and ruin my life) for me. It was difficult for me to admit that maybe I needed help, but I finally did, and just the fact of talking to an objective listener who wouldn't judge—but who just listened and sometimes advised—helped. In my opinion, anything that opens our inner selves to our selves and lets us know a little bit more about our selves than we did before is terrific.

Back to pleasuring others. Once you get your self straightened out physically and emotionally, you'll begin to *want* to do things for others. Warren Avis (founder of "We try harder" Avis Rent-A-Car), has written two books, *Shared Participation* and *The Art of Sharing,* and is finishing a new book, *The Avis Axiom,* which will be published shortly. He says:

When I was younger I was taught that true love was selfless, that it was so pure there was nothing for me. When one of my children made an accomplishment which I was proud of and I felt was solely for their good, I thought I was doing as great as I could do. Then I started to feel good and proud regarding their accomplishments and got guilt feelings and felt I was selfish because I was taught I shouldn't have any gratification. This in turn stops you from trying because gratification is sinful. You're not as good a father or mother, you think. Once you understand that fulfillment and gratification are part of love and are normal, natural and necessary (contrary to some religious teachings that true love is selfless), then you can easily focus on doing good deeds (which is caring), and be proud and happy that you helped bring them about. We are a pluralistic animal and our relations are always with other people. It's a necessity and a natural good desire to inter-relate with people.

What is the greatest gift we can give to another? Ralph Waldo Emerson says, "The only true gift is a portion of thyself." Warren says that love is "caring plus fulfillment," but I believe that the giving of love is automatically the fulfillment, and if you are able to trust in and give of yourself, that is heaven.

But giving love is only half the story. We must be able to receive love also. Clark Blackburn, who co-authored the book *How to Stay Married* and is the executive director of Family Service Association of America and himself a marriage counselor, says that sometimes a couple has different ideas about how love should be expressed, and this stops an intimate relationship from forming. If a husband feels he's expressing love by working hard all day and coming home, and feels loved if his wife has dinner waiting, but his wife feels that these things are duties and not expressions of love, and she needs shows of affection like kisses or small, inexpensive but thoughtful gifts, or an "I love you," only if they communicate their desires to each other will they ever find out how to pleasure each other. We sometimes assume that if the other person really loves us, he or she will sense what makes us happy, but this hardly ever happens. We must let our partner know what pleasures us (and what displeasures us), or we'll be frustrated forever waiting for Mr. or Ms. Right, who will automatically know what to do to make us happy. But it just doesn't happen this way. We have to talk and listen to each other before intimacy can grow.

And when your mate does make a special effort to show love in the way you want, always respond even if at the moment you don't feel like it. Receiving love is just as important as giving it. The moments of sharing on an emotional level will give you a feeling of closeness and security, and intimate relations are based on a security in each other, and when you have this security, you will open up more and give of yourself more.

Dr. Pierre Mornell, psychiatrist and author of *The Lovebook*, says that lovemaking is like a complex puzzle, and for many of us something is usually missing. We must share our hopes and dreams with our partner because, very often, couples forget about the excitement once shared by talking and planning the future, and those dreams will fill love with energy and fantasy. We must dream together, and share our hopes and fantasies. Your love life doesn't have to lose the thrill, as long as you're willing to replace whatever is missing with something both of you will find exciting.

So much of pleasure is mental, Dale Carnegie says:

> When dealing with people, let us remember we are
> not dealing with creatures of logic. We are dealing
> with creatures of emotion, creatures bustling with
> prejudices and motivated by pride and vanity.

I asked Warren Avis how he pleasures others, and
he says by giving gifts, telling funny stories, giving
compliments, dressing well, taking care of himself
—these all give pleasure to others.

One of the great pleasurings in life (and one of my
favorites) happens during that special emotional intimacy between two people who love each other
after they have made love—the communication, the
talking to each other about life in general or about
specific things which can range from chitchat to
"What kind of a relationship do you think Freud
really had with his wife?"

When feelings of love are flowing back and forth,
the communication is more open, the talking is freer
and very relaxed and fun. Even the heavy stuff is
fun when your feet are entwined.

And while we're on feet entwined, what about
hand-holding and hugging and just plain touching?
I'm a toucher. I like the feeling of skin (of course it
depends on whose), but I feel sorry for people who
never touch. It's an electricity thing—currents between people.

Animals love to be touched and petted. Seymour,
my dog, sometimes drives me crazy when he's in the
mood for petting. Often, when I'm reading, he'll
push his nose under my hand till his head is all the
way under my hand and I'll pet him a second and
take my hand away. He'll do it again and keep doing

it for as long as I'll put up with it. His record so far is about twenty minutes (I should say *my* record, because he could go on for hours). So if Seymour and all his friends dig being touched, I'm entitled.

Since I wrote the above about touching, I read an article in *Vogue* by Barbara Lang Stern called "You Need Body Contact With Others: It Satisfies 'Skin Hunger' ". It says:

> How do you feel about being hugged or held? Are there times you'd like to be touched or patted or stroked or cuddled more than you are? If so, you share a need or desire that is overlooked all too often in our culture today. In fact, a name has been given to the feeling of being starved for physical contact and affection: "skin hunger".

Ms. Stern also says that babies deprived of body contact and affection, even though all other physical needs are being met, may *fail to survive.* She quotes Arthur Burton and Louis Heller from their article "The Touching of the Body":

> Problems of discipline with children are often displaced needs for affection. This is commonly known. But what is not so well-known is that the child wants to be touched even at the cost of severe bodily punishment.

Ms. Stern notes that our skin is not only our largest organ, it's also our oldest, and it served as our first medium of communication, and that touch is our most fundamental and crucial sense.

It's good to know you crave it as much as I do, and every time I touch you I'll know I'm pleasuring you as much as me.

Pleasuring you is one of the things that makes life fun and exciting. Thinking up things to do is fun, and doing them is exciting because watching you enjoy pleasure gives me so much pleasure.

In reality, pleasuring you is pleasuring me!

Faith-full To You

WHAT'S THE DIFFERENCE between faithful and faith-full? When someone asks you if you've been faithful to your roomie or spouse, it means have you cheated on him or her, have you been sexually true and not fooled around?

When I use the word "faith-full," it means something infinitely more. It means do you believe in your roomie or spouse, are you full of faith in that person, are you convinced that he or she is a person with whom you can be vulnerable and open and trusting? Do you believe that person would never willingly and knowingly hurt you or take advantage of you?

There's a terrific ad campaign which has been running a while by De Beers Consolidated Mines, Ltd. One in particular caught my eye:

With this diamond we promise to always be friends.

To stay frank and honest with each other. And always bring things out in the open, where we can talk them over.

To never stop being sensitive to each other's needs.

And even after we're married, to always be there. Sometimes to give little pep talks. Sometimes just to listen.

That's the part of our love we don't ever want to lose. And this diamond is our promise that we never will.

If I have faith in you, if I believe in you, then you are my friend and I will not knowingly hurt you and I know that you will not knowingly hurt me. Sometimes a sexual attraction masks itself as friendship, but a friend wouldn't forget to call, or play hard-to-get, or even worse, play those other silly sexual games. A friend is someone who truly wants the best for me, who makes me aware of my "worthmoreness."

So the first thing I want in a relationship is a friend, someone who really cares for me and my feelings, because caring is love. Sure, you can tell me all you want how much you love me, but if you haven't seen me in a few days and you don't care enough to call just to see how I'm doing, then it's not love.

In *On Caring*, Milton Mayeroff says:

To care for someone, I must *know* many things. I must know, for example, who the other is, what his powers and limitations are, what his needs are, and what is conducive to his growth; I must know how to respond to his needs, and what my own powers and limitations are.

So if I believe in you and care for you, it isn't something that just happens, it's something that I create. Caring is very creative, like painting a picture or writing a poem—and it's fun. I believe *everything* in life should be fun, and if something doesn't seem like it would be fun, by becoming creative you *make* it fun—just like you would use your imagination to build a novel through ideas and words, or a house through ideas and blueprints, you build a loving relationship through ideas and caring.

Jerry Stiller and Anne Meara, besides being (in my opinion) the funniest comedy team in America, are the lovingest couple. They're not only loving to themselves but to everyone around them. Jerry loves Anne, Anne loves Jerry, and they both love everybody. But they really work at their marriage, and several years ago split as a comedy team because they felt it was destroying their personal relationship. The pressures of doing nightclub work and being constantly hilarious and being away from their two kids was bad for the whole family. So Anne did lots of TV on her own, on *Rhoda* and the *Kate McShane* series and Jerry starred in *The Ritz* on Broadway and in *Joe and Sons* on TV. Their radio commercials for Blue Nun, the wine company, are classics (they could continue working as a team on radio because it's easy to do and you don't have to travel). I love the one where Jerry asks her what kind of wine she would like and Anne says she doesn't know so Jerry asks if she'd like a little Blue

Nun, and Anne, in her delicious Brooklyn accent, says, "Look, I don't want a miracle, I just want some wine."

Jerry and Anne's marriage, is to them, the most important thing in their lives, and they'll do anything to protect it and that's why it's so successful —because they work at it (but everything they do is fun!).

There's a wonderful book called *No-Fault Marriage* by Marcia Lasswell and Norman M. Lobsenz, and in it they talk about intimacy:

> A man and woman may be close to each other physically and still remain emotional strangers. Yet to lock away one's thoughts and feelings is to deprive a partner of the most significant gift one can offer—the truest kind of intimacy.
>
> Sexual difficulties are reported by four out of every five couples that marriage counselors see. While there may be other causes, a surprising amount of this sexual unhappiness grows directly out of the fear of intimacy. For these people, sex may be good early in marriage. But when they realize that a good marriage demands ever-higher degrees of closeness and emotional commitment, then there may be a retreat from sex.
>
> Sexual "distancing" often goes with a general absence of marital intimacy. Its crisis symptom may be infidelity—which most of the time is not so much a search for sex as it is for emotional intimacy. A couple who can face that fact, and do something about it, has a good chance not only to survive the infidelity but to grow closer.
>
> Intimacy inevitably brings vulnerability. Suppose

we get hurt? Suppose we are rejected?

Retreating from intimacy is no guarantee that you will not be hurt anyway—by someone, somehow. In the long run, reaching out and opening up is not only less risky—it is infinitely more rewarding.

Intimacy is that delicious sharing of secrets, maybe not all of them (because there's always a tiny part of us we reserve for ourselves alone), but most of them. Shouldn't a friend know all about us? And love us anyway? If we're scared to let a friend know our so-called "bad things," then we don't trust that friend, and without trust there can never be real friendship or closeness.

Again, Milton Mayeroff:

> If another person is to grow through my caring, he must trust me, for only then will he open himself to me and let me reach him. Without trust in me, he will be defensive and closed. . . .
>
> Trusting the other is to let go; it includes an element of risk and a leap into the unknown, both of which take courage.

Now what relationship connotes the utmost in trust? The biggest commitment we can make is marriage. Sure we trust our pals, but only to a degree. In marriage we form a bond that makes us a team. As a team, there are two of us against the world, which in a good marriage makes us ten times as strong. You can be strong where I'm weak and I can be strong where you're weak. We complement each other and our team can be invincible. But we must trust. That's the single most important quality needed for loving. If I'm afraid of you, I can't love you. I can be terribly attracted to you physically, I can "fall madly in love" with you, we can rise to the heights of passion together, but I can't love you. If I'm afraid of you I can't trust you and if I can't trust you I can't be open and vulnerable, which is necessary to love. You may turn me on and we may have a great affair, but the intimacy needed for a great relationship will be missing, and certainly if we're married and the trust is missing, the days of the marriage are numbered.

Lots of people think that marriage is on the way out, that living together without a license is going to take over, but all the facts dispute this. People need marriage and want the security and emotional strength it gives. Dr. Clara G. Livsey, assistant professor of psychiatry at Johns Hopkins University, says that with all the problems people have with their health, their professions, money, or their kids, they are able to cope if they have the strength given them by a good marriage. Dr. Livsey explains that marriages fall apart because people don't listen to each other. They lose the line of communication, and when that happens, trust starts eroding.

Psychologist Dr. Jon D. Boller believes that a marriage certificate is vital to a good, lasting relationship, even though many free-thinking live-togethers look down on it as a mere piece of paper (a driver's license, a birth certificate, a passport, a mortgage—each is a mere piece of paper, but very difficult to exist without). Many studies show that couples who live together are confused about their roles and feel irresponsible toward the relationship. They don't feel a responsibility because there aren't the legal binds on them. People who live together have no "role model." Dr. Linda Budd, family social scientist at the University of Minnesota, believes that live-togethers act like married people (they're copying married couple roles), but they don't have the same commitment. Most people today, as always, believe in marriage, consciously or subconsciously, and eventually do get married.

It's incredible how many people think that marriage is only good and necessary for women, but that men don't really need it. There's that awful cliché about "the woman chasing the man until he catches her." Jessie Bernard's book *The Future of Marriage* disputes this, and it's a fascinating study.

> Traditionally, men consider marriage a trap for themselves and a prize for their wives. Statistically, marriage is good for men—physically, socially, and psychologically.
>
> Traditionally, all women want to marry, and most want to become mothers. Statistically, childless marriages are happier; and marriage, literally, makes thousands of women sick.

She goes on.

> Men, in brief, have been railing against marriage for centuries. If marriage were actually as bad for men as it has been painted by them, it would long since have lost any future it may ever have had. In the face of all the attacks against it, the vitality of marriage has been

quite stupendous. Men have cursed it, aimed barbed witticisms at it, denigrated it, bemoaned it—and never ceased to want and need it or to profit from it.

There are few findings more consistent, less equivocal, more convincing than the sometimes spectacular and always impressive superiority on almost every index—demographic, psychological, or social—of married over never-married men. Despite all the jokes about marriage in which men indulge, all the complaints they lodge against it, it is one of the greatest boons of their sex. Employers, bankers, and insurance companies have long since known this. And whether they know it or not, men need marriage more than women do.

The actions of men with respect to marriage speak far louder than words; they speak, in fact, with a deafening roar. Once men have known marriage, they can hardly live without it. Most divorced and widowed men remarry. At every age, the marriage rate for both divorced and widowed men is higher than the rate for single men. Half of all divorced white men who remarry do so within three years after divorce. Indeed, it might not be farfetched to conclude that *the verbal assaults on marriage indulged in by men are a kind of compensatory reaction to their dependence on it.*

The reason this book is so interesting to me is that unless both men and women realize their desire and need for marriage, they both won't work to make it successful. If men use the "out" that they really didn't want to be married in the first place, or that they really don't need to be married, then they won't make any exertion to make it work. Because there are two involved, it takes two to make it work.

Two to communicate, two to care for each other, two to trust in each other, not just one. If only one works at it, it's doomed to fail. Of course, not only some men have a negative attitude toward marriage, but some women do too. However, the majority certainly seems to be men.

So, once we acknowledge our need for a loving relationship in marriage, we can try to solve the problems instead of running away from them and imagining that right around the corner we'll meet the man or woman of our dreams and we'll live happily ever after.

There is a definite trend toward fidelity which is strengthening marriages, and people are returning to the old-fashioned marital virtues. Dr. Carlfred Broderick, sociologist and head of the marriage and family counseling center at USC, believes that no matter how terrific someone is in bed, there is just no way a person can feel deep affection in one-night stands. He says, based on clinical experience, that people are disillusioned with sexually open marriages and are discovering that you don't run away to happiness—you build it in marriage. Dr. Broderick says that couples are learning to talk over their problems with each other instead of looking around outside of marriage for the answers, that people are getting tired of tricking themselves into thinking that the next conquest will be the magic one, and are focusing on deeper involvement with their mate instead of looking around.

Dr. Arthur Weider, assistant clinical professor of medical psychology at Columbia University College of Physicians and Surgeons, says that people are definitely beginning to work on the marriage they have rather than looking around for outside stimulation, and Dr. Leslie Rabkin, a psychologist, says that intimacy is what people want and that infidelity causes pain and marital breakups.

As French novelist Honoré de Balzac said:

> It is easier to be a lover than a husband, for the same reason that it is more difficult to be witty every day than to say bright things only occasionally.

There's a very good book out called *Learning to Love Again* by Mel Krantzler. In it he talks about separating the past from the present, making relationships grow, the why of what happened in a breakup, making the connection between sex and love, and many other terrific ideas. There's one quote I particularly like:

> Sex is an expression of intimacy and trust in a committed relationship. Promiscuity wipes out the trust that exists.

Mature love (and you can be mature at eighteen and immature at eighty—age has nothing to do with it), the commitment to build a life with each other and for each other, is one of the most beautiful experiences of marriage. Love is sharing the pleasant and not-so-pleasant experiences and being supportive in every phase of marriage. When a couple gives total support to one another, a deep bond of love forms between them. Loyalty is terribly important in marriage. It's hard to trust a disloyal person.

There are lots of ways to back your husband, wife or roomie—when he or she is down because of a business setback, you can boost self-esteem by your loyal support. When your partner is in an argument, don't pipe up for the other side, even if you disagree or feel the other person is right.

It's easy to smile or be supportive when everything is going along perfectly, but when loyalty really counts is when things start going awry. Sure, you can disagree when the two of you are alone and you talk something through, but when you're with a party of people or even just one other person, defend your spouse, or at least don't disagree. And if you're the one who needs support, it's important to be able to accept it. Don't reject your partner's help and try to carry your burden alone. Love is sharing everything—the good and the bad.

I'd like to go back to Professor Dorothy Tennov and her thoughts of limerence, or romantic love. She says that exclusivity is a major characteristic of limerence:

> The limerent person wants the limerent object, and no one else. You can't be limerent over two people— only one at a time.
>
> In order to be assured of this exclusivity, a limerent often craves some kind of commitment. A ring, a promise the loved will never go out with anyone else. The need for commitment is so strong that people in the limerent state promise even when they know they shouldn't. I found a quote that describes this dilemma perfectly: "Love is what makes a person who is philosophically opposed to monogamous sexual relation-

ships on the grounds that jealousy and possessiveness are not part of human nature but simply the by-products of a decadent capitalist society, take it all back."

Carl R. Rogers believes that love should never be smothering:

". . . the degree to which I can create relationships which facilitate the growth of others as separate persons is a measure of the growth I have achieved in myself . . ."

A happy marriage is the ideal state, but it sure seems difficult to attain. I don't know many really happily married couples, but the few I do know make me believe that with love and thought and work (most people will knock themselves out eight hours a day at their jobs, but they don't think work is necessary for a relationship, which in my opinion, is more important than a job; you can usually find another job more quickly than another good relationship), two people *can* find happiness for a lifetime together. One couple has been married twenty-eight years and they still have fun together. The other day Laura, my happily married friend, told me that her husband Matty tells her often that if he had it to do all over again, he'd marry her in a second. Now, *that's* romantic!

Another sensational married couple who adore each other are Mitzi Gaynor and Jack Bean. They've been married twenty-five years and you'd think they got married last week. They need each other (what happened to needing each other?), but more importantly, they like each other. Every year Mitzi and Jack travel all over the country doing the summer theater circuit with her super-colossal musical act which her husband produces and oversees. Jack is always with Mitzi and Mitzi is always with Jack because that's the way they want it. When she does her yearly TV special, Jack does everything for her but perform. They both are incredibly funny people and maybe it's their shared sense of humor that makes their marriage such fun, but whatever it is, they are living proof that not only can a union of two people work for many years, it can get better with time. They say they're more in love now than they were twenty-five years ago, and they act it. I was talking to Jack recently about their beautiful Beverly Hills home and asked if he would ever sell it, or if he had too great an emotional tie to it, and he said, "The house, the cars mean nothing to me. My only emotional tie is Mitzi. She's the only thing I really care about."

Recently, at a party, I met Sloan Wilson, the super-novelist who wrote *The Man In the Gray Flannel Suit* and the current best-seller *Ice Brothers*, with many other terrific books in between. He was at the party with his lovely wife, Betty, who made me feel great when she told me she'd been on my Dynamite Milkshake ever since she'd bought my last book. Then I met Jessica, their pretty daughter, and we all got into a lively conversation about writers, vitamins and life in general. Sloan and Betty have been married seventeen years and you can tell they're still in love. He told me, "Life without my wife would be worse than life lived standing on one leg. I couldn't exist without Betty—she's my partner in every area. She's my emotional partner, my physical partner and my business partner. She handles all the business details I don't have time for. In fact, if I had to do all the business things, I wouldn't have time to write. Betty takes all the burdens off me so I can concentrate totally on my work. Without her I would have no efficiency, no comfort and no joy." Then I read Sloan's "author bio" on the jacket of *Small Town,* and he says it all there:

> Although it may sound sentimental, the only real meaning I have found in life has been in my wife and children. Without them I would be in more despair than a bankrupt millionaire.

Superstar singer Helen Reddy and her manager-husband Jeff Wald have never believed that either of them has to choose between family life and a career. Helen has a teenage daughter by her first marriage and she and Jeff have a young son together, and they both work hard and travel a lot, but try to spend as much time as they can with their family. When she plays Vegas, she jets back and forth every day so she can spend time with the two kids. Helen and Jeff are very much in love and have been together since 1966, and when Helen wrote and sang "I Am Woman" in 1972, that was the spurt she needed to boost her to superstardom. They both say that the marriage is the most important thing in their lives and they'll always work hard to make it a good one because to them it's a lifetime commitment.

The Bee Gees are a great rock group, and their *Saturday Night Fever* album is my favorite so far. All four of them, Barry, Robin, Maurice and Andy, are very family-oriented, and like living close to each other. Marriage is important to all of them—they think family because their mother, Barbara, an ex-singer, and father Hugh, a bandleader on a ferryboat in England, raised them to be a close-knit family that believes in marriage and family life.

Lola and Robert Redford have been happily married more than twenty years, and family life is important to both of them. They have three kids, and they divide their time between New York, where they own a large Fifth Avenue co-op, and their ranch home in Provo, Utah. Lola and Robert make sure that twice every year they spend a couple of weeks alone, just driving around the West, renewing their love and friendship. They are a romantic, loving couple who truly care for each other and for the world around them.

Gladys Shelly is a beautiful, loving person who's written many terrific songs ("My World Is You", "Clown Town") including one of the greatest torch songs of all time, "How Did He Look?" She and her late husband, Irving Rosenthal (who owned and operated Palisades Amusement Park, which used to be just across the George Washington Bridge from New York), were happily married for over twenty-five years. Gladys tells how they delighted in pleasuring each other. "Every morning he made breakfast and brought it to me in bed. And the night before, I always packed a brown bag for his lunch even though he had over thirty-five eating places at

Palisades, just so he could have a really nutritious meal. Our greatest pleasure was doing things for each other."

The late Jacqueline Susann was the most famous novelist ever (and the only one to hit Number One on all the best-seller lists with three books in a row), and she was a beautiful and sweet woman. I knew Jackie and her husband, Irving Mansfield, and they had a perfect marriage for all of their thirty-two years together. I asked Irving about why and how it was such a smash success when the majority of marriages around aren't. He said, "Where was I going to find a better wife—she was clever, good-looking, very funny, charitable, kind, easy to get along with—everything I'd ever want in another person? If I ever went to a coed college, I'd want to be her roommate." Then I asked him what made him such a terrific husband, and he said he was always very considerate of Jackie—he always remembered her birthday, her mother's birthday, their anniversary. And even going back to their wedding day, when he didn't have much money, he went out and put all his savings of $600 as a down payment on a $3,200 mink coat for his bride. Now *that's* love (it's easier when you've got lots of money). Irving paraphrased Freud: "You attract and get a response and create a bond." Their bond lasted for thirty-two years because they not only loved each other, they constantly showed each other how much.

Howard Cosell was a practicing lawyer who gave that up to become the most well-known sportscaster in America, and has been "telling it like it is" ever since. He's now one of the most listened-to voices in the country, and even though so many people who don't know him don't like him, he's one of the nicest people I've ever met. In fact, when I did his nationally syndicated radio show, he knocked himself out to give me a terrific interview because he's a sweet and kind man who really does care. Howard's been married for over thirty years to Mary Edith, and they both really care for each other and work at having what Howard considers "my most important success." He believes, as does his wife, that love is the only important thing, and that love will always surpass sex, but that some people unfortunately think that sex is more important. Howard says that people needing each other is more important than *anything,* and that nowadays it seems like people are afraid of needing each other. He says love will overcome all obstacles, but love has to be nurtured, like any other thing. If you don't water your plant and give it sunshine, it will die. If you don't feed and exercise your dog, it will die. And love needs attention too. Howard and Mary Edith give lots of it to each other.

Doctor Neil Solomon and I became good friends several years ago when we appeared together on a TV show in Washington, D.C., and then later on other TV shows. He was, until recently, Secretary of Health and Mental Hygiene for the State of Maryland. He's now a syndicated columnist in over one hundred newspapers, has just filmed a pilot for a TV show called *Take Care* (and I appeared as his first guest), besides, of course, being a very well-known doctor, specializing in weight control and allergies. He's authored several best-selling books, and *The Truth About Weight Control*, which is his most widely read book so far, has reached millions of people. Neil and his beautiful wife, Frema, have been married almost twenty-five years and are really happily mated. They believe in togetherness and practice it. When Neil had his local TV show in Baltimore, *Prescription For Family Health*, Frema produced it; working together like that is a true test of love.

The love of Walter Cronkite's life is his darling wife Betsy, and they've been happily married for over thirty years. They have a great emotional partnership and they do as many things as they can together. One of their greatest pleasures is sailing together and they do it as often as they can when the weather permits. Walter loves the sea, and because of this he's become very active in ecological studies of the ocean. He traveled extensively and put together a TV special on the oceans and seas because he's worried that eventually we will ruin all our natural resources and kill all our fish if we don't stop our wanton destruction soon. Walter cares for Betsy and for all life around him and it shows.

Otto Preminger has been happily married over twenty years to his beautiful Hope and says he's always believed strongly in marriage, but not always is a person lucky enough to find the right person the first time around, or even sometimes the second time. But finding that person (and he quotes Shakespeare) is a "consummation devoutly to be wished."

Frank Gifford strongly believes in being faithful

to your mate—he says otherwise it's not your mate. He says he needs a lot of attention—that he's lived without it, but finds life much more fun with it and with sharing accomplishments with someone he cares for—his wife Astrid. Frank loves being married, and says that "marriage is the best way to share everything."

Several years ago I was in the middle of a falling-apart relationship and we desperately needed guidance to try to save our marriage (or see if it could be saved). Over a period of several years we saw two marriage counselors, two psychologists and one hypnotist-psychologist (you can't say I'm not determined!). Then I was truly fortunate to meet an outstanding psychiatrist, Dr. Helen Singer Kaplan. Now there are lots of very good counselors around, and as I said, I've met a few, but Dr. Kaplan is so outstanding that I'd like to tell a little about her. It was a very trying time (as it always is) and Helen immediately told me the story of the breakup of *her* marriage, which she had been through not too long before, and how traumatic it was for her. I loved her for having the courage to tell me how she had suffered and what she had been through. It's not easy to admit having failed at something as important as your marriage (don't I know!). She told me some of the details, and just knowing that this brilliant and beautiful woman surmounted her pain, put her broken marriage behind her, and went on to find a new and stronger love made me feel terrific and very optimistic (she remarried several months after I met her). Being an extremely perceptive woman, she knew very soon after our first meeting that there wasn't a chance that my marriage could work. I had tried against insurmountable problems to make the relationship work because I never like to give up but sometimes giving up something, after you've done all you can, gains you much, much more—and the peace of mind the final split brought to me made me know immediately that Dr. Kaplan was right. Real love, in a positive relationship, always grows and makes you feel good. A negative relationship brings tension, stress and much unhappiness.

Dr. Kaplan has been written about in many magazine articles. And one quote from *Harper's Bazaar* in particular I love,

> Most people would probably be happiest in a gentle, committed, intimate relationship that is also sexually satisfying. I think human beings are a bonding species —not all species are. Some species bond for only half an hour during the mating season; others for a lifetime. We have no way of knowing what our natural bonding pattern is—what we are actually programmed for—because economic and social pressures have always demanded lifetime bonding . . . .

She goes on to say:

> But my guess—and it is only a guess—would be that most people are comfortable as married couples.

As difficult as it is to have a happy marriage, it's almost as difficult to be a "successful single." Dr. Terry Richards is a psychologist who works a great deal with single couples, and he says that just because they're single, it doesn't mean they're having a terrific time. The one thing successful singles have is a high self-esteem, and they work at promoting themselves in interpersonal relationships and developing lots of friends and lovers. Unsuccessful singles are alienated, fearful of being taken advantage of and see others as "things" to be acquired. They tend to be cynical about money. Men use money to impress and acquire women and women seek out men with money. Some singles are securely monogamous and are very like marrieds with their own interests and friends. Non-monogamous singles like new relationships which they find sexually stimulating, but often experience anxiety related to performance. Unsuccessful singles have no communication so they can't express their needs, and they wander from person to person, never connecting. Of course, this happens to some married, too. Dr. Richards believes that it's really up to both parties to make a good and joint relationship, to have a balance between sharing and the energy of outside interests. He says that so few people let themselves love or be loved and they never know the joy of sharing love. He says this isn't something that is easily changed—it takes hard work, but that the results are worth it.

So if I'm faith-full to you and you're faith-full to me, if we truly believe in each other and in ourselves, we will not only be an invincible team, we will individually grow to be stronger, more productive selves, and when that happens, our love for each other will grow, our love for every other human being will grow, and our love for ourselves will grow, and then we will know, not think or believe, but KNOW, that heaven *is* the condition of those who can love.

Afterword

Now that you've read the book, you've found out all about my thoughts and feelings on love. Now I'd like you to find out all about *your* thoughts and feelings.

I'd like you to ask yourself a few questions:

1. Do you feel terrific physically, mentally and emotionally?

    —enough so you feel really energetic yet relaxed most of the time?

    —enough so that you're full of enthusiasm about all the things you're doing at work and at home?

2. Are you pleasuring yourself?

    —enough so that you feel you really *are* getting as much of the pleasure in life as you should be getting?

    —enough so that your love life is booming?

3. Are you being faith-full to yourself?

    —enough so that you really believe strongly in

yourself and in all the things you're doing?

—enough so that you never put yourself down for any so-called mistakes, but you know that whatever you did was for a reason and if it didn't turn out the way you wanted it to, that *also* is for a reason—that of your self-growth?

4. Do you believe that you have a Source which is the beginning of *everything* you do?

—enough that you honestly don't worry about the future or regret anything about the past because you know your Source is taking care of it all?

—enough that you dare to take positive chances in your work or career, trusting that your Source is always with you and that if you trust it enough, you'll always make the right decision?

5. Do you know the sensational feeling of being adored?

—enough that you can call it to mind whenever you want to feel a warm glow in the memory of it?

—enough so that that memory gives you such a feeling of warmth that you want to spread it to others?

6. Do you use the word "love" with people and not only just with inanimate objects?

—enough so that you can interchange it with the word "like"?

—enough so that you say "I love you" to everyone close to you?

7. Do you feel that you are or could one day be a really great lover?

—enough that you know that you honestly do care for all creatures, great and small, and all other things existing, and in this knowledge know that you don't ever want to hurt *any* of them?

—enough that people respond to you in a positive way reflecting your love for them?

8. Do you pleasure other people?

—enough to feel that you really like most people and love to see them happy and know that you're responsible?

—enough so that the smiles on their faces let you know that you've made them happier?

9. Are you faith-full to other people?

—enough that your belief in them makes them feel better about themselves?

—enough to know that you really are a positive force in other people's lives, which then makes your life more positive?

1. How important is feeling terrific to you? Are you willing to try the Dynamite Milkshake and vites to change your body for the better? How important is having super energy to you? Energy to do all the things you've wanted to do but were too pooped to even try, energy to begin all the projects you've been dreaming about for so long you can't even remember, energy to finish all the projects you started and then left in midstream because you were too weak and tired to finish them. How important is getting rid of tension and anxiety? Tension that gives you headaches, backaches, stomach aches, neck aches, chest pains, canker sores in your mouth,

itches all over your body, acne all over your face;
anxiety that makes you want to scream, fills you
with fear about ridiculous things, makes you think
you're going crazy, makes your psyche feel frazzled
all the time. How important is getting rid of depression? Depression that makes you feel draggy all the
time, makes you cry a lot over silly things, makes
you feel everybody else is better than you, makes
you feel that life isn't worth living, makes you wonder why you were born.

Are you willing to try the Dynamite Milkshake
and vites right away and test it for just a month?
The worst thing that could happen is you've spent
five minutes a day mixing the shake and laying out
the vites, and the best thing that could happen is you
get rid of all your physical problems when you
straighten out your body chemistry. If you've got
any physical problem (from being fat to having pimples or acne and pains), it's a sign that your body
chemistry is imbalanced, and the shake and vites
will balance out your chemical imbalance. Your
body can't talk to you—the most it can do to tell you
you're doing something wrong is to become sick, or
fat, or break out in pimples. It's up to you to
straighten it out.

When you try the Dynamite Milkshake and test
it for a month, prepare yourself to feel sensational.
Get ready for the energy to do a lot more than
you're doing now. Say good-by to feeling rotten and
depressed. Get set to join the Y or a health club or
buy a tennis racquet or get some jogging shoes.
Once you start feeling terrific, your body's going to

want to move a lot more, it will need a lot more action than it's getting now.

So try the Dynamite Milkshake and vites and give it a whirl for a month and you'll be hooked for life.

Get ready to become super-charged and bursting with energy.

2.   How important is having fun and getting all the pleasure you can out of life? Are you willing to take some time out of your busy schedule and concentrate only on your self? To slow your frantic pace and recharge your psyche, to pull all your forces together and unify your body, your mind and your emotions so that you can be one strong, whole person. How important is a happy sex life to you? Are you willing to agree that between two consenting persons who care for each other, anything goes? That guilt should never, *ever* be tolerated because there's nothing to be guilty about? Are you willing to look at sex as a body function like eating, drinking and sleeping, and realize that only in excess or deficiency (as in all things), can anything but good happen? Stuffing yourself with food or starving your body are both equally bad. Are you willing to see sex as a function of the body necessary to physical health? Sex is one of life's greatest sources of happiness and it should be understood and used as a release of physical, mental and emotional tension, between two people who care for each other. When you pleasure someone else you will find you are also pleasuring yourself.

3.   How important is believing in yourself and believing that you can attain all the goodies that you've always wanted? Are you willing to start a

mental diet and deliberately keep out all the negative thoughts that creep into your mind and limit you in everything you do? Do you think you can make an honest effort to stay away from negative people who drag you down, and concentrate only on positive people in your life? If someone in your life close to you is feeding you negs, can you split temporarily or tune out until you get strong enough to figure out how to handle him or her? How important is a strong, positive self-image to you? Are you willing to take a few minutes a day—you can start with one minute—and do some mental exercises that will slowly change your belief in yourself from negative to positive? Will you start to train your self to tune out every time a negative downer about your self enters your mind? Just tune out the negative—no matter what it is, refuse to accept it, keep your mind blank and refuse to let any thought in. Hang on and just keep your mind a blank. Once you are able to do this and to show your mind that *you're* the boss and not vice versa, then you can control your mind and make it think about something positive that you want to be or that you want to do. Your self-image is exactly that—a *self* image, created by you. So if, when you were a non-thinking child, you were programmed by your parents or teachers or some other adults to think badly of yourself, now you can change those negative thoughts. You as a child accepted their opinions of you, but now that you're a thinking adult, you can reject their negative opinions, throw them out, and replace them with positive feelings which you are starting to have about your self.

Once you are in control of your mind, you can dictate exactly what *you* want your mind to accept.

Are you willing to try?

4. How important is your feeling that you are never alone, that your Giant Self is your only real Source and is always with you? Are you willing to push out all thoughts of fear (which disguise themselves sometimes as anger, hostility, jealousy, envy, and all the other negative feelings), and replace them with thoughts of love?

The thoughts of love must start with your self first, and after that you can't help caring for others because you'll be happy.

Are you willing to believe that God or Spirit or Love or Source or *Something* created you, and She/He/It is intelligent and cares enough for you to have created you, and if this is true, then don't you feel that you should take terrific care of your self too?

But you can't give something that isn't there, so to put love into your life, you must first learn to care for your self, and when that happens there will be enough love inside you to spread around to everyone and everything that comes into your life.

Are you willing to try to love yourself? To make sure your body is healthy and work at it as much as you work at your job, because it's much more important than any job you could ever have. Start to think about yourself—become introspective. Don't be afraid of asking yourself questions about yourself. Believe me, your Giant Self or Source knows what you need and will give it to you if you'll only listen. You spend so much time on other people and things—spend some time on your self.

Selfmoreness, not selflessness. If God or your Giant Self or your Source thinks enough of you to have put you here, then you must be something special (we're all unique in our own special way—there's no one in the whole world who's exactly like me or you).

Be special to your self.

Are you willing to try?

5.   How important is being loved to you? Are you willing to accept love from others because you've been loving to them and love begets love? Everything in life is cause and effect, and when you love others, truly love them, they will love you back. And being loved, feeling loved, is the warmest, most gratifying and satisfying feeling in the whole world. Even the most self-sufficient people need to feel loved and wanted and needed. And when you can recall this feeling whenever you want, it can be a great source of strength for you. You cannot feel hassled and loved at the same time. Feelings can only be experienced one at a time, so if you can train yourself to recall the sense memory of being loved and try to keep it with you, it will help make your life a positive one, and a lot more fun.

6.   How important is love in your life? Are you willing to put it above all else and make it important in everything you do? Whether you're a cop or a beautician, you can make love a part of your job. You can smile more, and try to control your temper if something upsets you, and just be all-around more pleasant.

At the beginning of the book I quoted Dostoevsky

who said, "Hell is the condition of those who cannot love," and then I quoted myself: "Heaven is the condition of those who *can* love," but maybe I should have said that heaven is the condition of those who *will* love. "Can" means able to, and "will" means an act of the will. We're all *able* to love, it's just that we don't all *will* to love, for whatever reasons we might have. If we don't will "to love," then we will "not to love," and if we are able to do that, then we can will "*to* love."

Just knowing that it's a conscious decision to start acting in a loving way makes it easier. We don't have to look for psychological reasons and uncover the past, or our childhood, to act loving. You don't have to feel tremendous surges of love to smile at someone or act courteously or not act obnoxiously or snap someone's head off. All we have to do is make the decision to try to smile more and be kinder to our fellow humans. We're all in this together and we might as well make it as much fun as we can, and smiling is a good first step.

7.   How important is being a great lover to you? Are you willing to try, really try, to appreciate everything around you and to see the beauty in all of God's creations? Although we all think of sex when we think of being a great lover, sex is only a small part of it. When we are able to love animals and sunsets and paintings and music and trees and flowers and furniture and buildings and cars and food and our bodies and our minds and our feelings —then and only then will we be great lovers—great lovers of *everything*. Sex is a part of everything, so to be a great lover, we must love sex too. But not more

nor less than all the others. When you have love in your heart, it's the same love for all things. True, it can be in different degrees (I love sunflower seeds more than walnuts, but I still love walnuts), but love for one thing is love for all things. If I love you then I must love all people. If I don't love all people, then I can't love you. I may need you, or be physically attracted to you, but unless I have love for all people and all things, then I can't love you.

So to be a great lover, start appreciating all things, and keep your mind and heart open—don't close off from anything. Try to see and appreciate the good in all things and love them all in different ways, and that love will rebound back to you, which will make you even *more* loving, and on it goes. Love that you give, brings back more love which increases your love and so you give more. The beauty part about love is that you can't ever run out of it. The more you give, the more you get.

8.   How important is having fun with other people and bringing pleasure to them? Are you willing to try to pleasure others by giving of your warmth and affection even though it might not be easy for you to do and you might not feel like it's worth it? At least if you try you'll find out if it's difficult or not and you'll find out if it's worth it or not. You might find out the castle you've been living in with the moat around it has a drawbridge that hasn't been used for such a long time that it's all rusty and squeaky, and when you lower it, even for a quickie, you might find that the caring that comes across it brings you a feeling that you'd forgotten even existed.

The drawbridge is your hand, your laughter, your understanding, and once that reaches others, and you feel the warmth and understanding that'll come back to you, you may never put the draw-bridge up again.

9. How important is believing in other people and making them feel confident about themselves and about everything they do? Are you willing to totally stop criticizing other people and finding fault with whatever they're doing? Sure, being an instant critic is easy, a lot easier than finding the positive, and sticking only to that. Being a critic is negative; when you criticize others, I guarantee you'll criticize yourself too, and who needs that? "Judge not that you be not judged" really means that. If you judge others, you'll judge yourself, and it's good-by spontaneity, good-by fun. You can't have fun when you're constantly watching yourself and watching others and monitoring everything. And when you think that people can't do certain things, or shouldn't do certain things, you limit yourself, because if they shouldn't do them, you'll think you shouldn't do them either. Like if you say you think singles bars are awful and you wouldn't be caught dead in one of them and the kind of peo-ple who go there are losers, etc., etc., and one night a couple of your friends are going to one, and want you to come along, and you've got nothing to do that night and you're bored and don't want to stay home alone—well, how can you go and have a good time when you've been such a knocker? So stop being a critic and start being a doer (critics are *never* doers

—they use all their energy criticizing, while doers are too busy *doing* to be critics).

So if you want to be a positive force in your own and other people's lives, make up your mind to begin. And the first step is to find something good and positive about everyone you meet, and don't just stop at that—*tell* the person how much you like or appreciate the positive quality he or she has. You'll make that person feel better about him- or herself, and you'll feel better for having done it.

Appendix I:
Vites & the Dynamite Milkshake

THE DYNAMITE Milkshake can be drunk as your total breakfast like I do (it's two big glasses and *very* filling) or as your total lunch, or you can drink half for breakfast and half for lunch, or half for lunch and half before bed—any way you want as long as you get four heaping tablespoons of Dynamite Milkshake in two glasses of skim milk every day. I personally love it as my total breakfast to start my day off, but to each his own. A friend of mine lost over twenty pounds by skipping breakfast and having half Dynamite Milkshake for lunch and half for dinner. It worked for him, but I don't recommend skipping breakfast unless you've never eaten food in the morning and feel you just can't hack it so you'll take it later. Getting the Dynamite Milkshake into your system at the start of the day is awfully important. But my friend was desperate

and felt he needed extreme measures to lose weight.
Now that he's lost it, and is gorgeous again, he's
keeping it off by taking half the Dynamite Milkshake for breakfast and half for lunch.

Here's the recipe for those who'd rather make the
Dynamite Milkshake from scratch than buy it
ready-made:

Buy powdered nutritional yeast, torula yeast or
brewer's yeast, which has calcium and magnesium
added and has a balance of the B vites on the label:
for instance, vitamin B1, 4 mg, vitamin B2, 4 mg,
vitamin B6, 4 mg. There are several brands on the
market and they can usually be found in most health
food stores. Next buy a jar of granulated lecithin, (if
you don't like the taste of the yeast or lecithin, try
another brand when you've finished the one you
bought—each brand is a little different).

I've made several minor changes (for example, I
found maple flavor better than vanilla), but basically
the shake and vites are the same Dynamite as ever.

NAURA'S DYNAMITE MILKSHAKE

Into a blender pour:

2 cups skimmed milk
1 tablespoon safflower oil
2 packets (or equivalent) of any sugar substitute
1 teaspoon maple flavor

Start the blender on low and add:

½ teaspoon powdered yeast (working up to four

heaping tablespoons—it takes about 4 weeks to slowly work up to the full amount)
4 heaping tablespoons lecithin.

Stop blender, cover, and put in fridge overnight (the overnight cold, for some reason, changes the taste of yeast from awful to good). Next morning put blender on high and whip till foamy for about thirty seconds.

When finished drinking, wash out blender, make tomorrow's batch and put in the fridge till next morning.

IMPORTANT

When you start out, be sure to use only ½ teaspoon yeast for the first couple of days, then go to 1 teaspoon, then 2 teaspoons, then 1 tablespoon, then 1 heaping tablespoon, etc, till you reach 4 heaping tablespoons (about four weeks).

You start right out with 4 heaping tablespoons of lecithin.

If you want a thinner milkshake, add more skim milk.

If you make the shake yourself, you may need digestive enzymes to help digest the powerful ingredients, and if so, take several with the shake.

If you buy it ready-made, the digestive enzymes (papaya) are already mixed in.

VITAMINS TO TAKE

Buy:

Vitamin A—2,500 units
Vitamin C—1,000 mgs. ascorbic acid
Vitamin D—400 units natural
Vitamin E—400 units mixed tocopherols
Dolomite (calcium and magnesium)

Every morning (with Dynamite Milkshake) take:

1 Vitamin A
2 Vitamin C
2 Vitamin D
1 Vitamin E
10 Dolomite pills (or put 1 heaping teaspoon dolomite powder in your milkshake)

Every evening (after dinner) take:

1 Vitamin A
2 Vitamin C
2 Vitamin D
1 Vitamin E
10 Dolomite pills (or put 1 heaping teaspoon dolomite powder in any liquid)

In my "Energy" book I gave the basics about vitamins, but now I'd like to go into a little more detail about why you need them and how many you should take. Before I found out about vitamins I was as confused as anyone about how many to take and which ones I needed. I used to take a multi-vitamin once a day and thought I was getting everything I needed, but now that I've studied and found out a lot about vites, I know I wasn't getting anywhere near as many as I needed. Every body is individual and has individual needs. We don't all need the same amounts of vites. What I've done is list what I believe is the minimum amount for *every body* (I take much more, which I'll tell you about later). Some of you may need more like I do, but I'll tell you how you will know if you're getting enough or need more.

Let's start with Vitamin A. Vitamins A and D are the only two vitamins you could take too much of, but that would be such a massive dose that I don't believe any rational person would take it. It would be like the doctor telling you to take two aspirins and you decided to take twenty (between forty and sixty aspirins are lethal). Too much A or D could have side effects, but again, you would have to take wildly excessive doses, and even then, according to *The Vitamins in Medicine* by F. Bicknell and F. Prescott, if you have enough Vitamin C in your system, it will counteract any toxicity. Most drugs, even the over-the-counter, non-prescription drugs, have a surprising toxicity, and of course prescription drugs are generally much more toxic. Drugs are foreign substances not usually found in the body, whereas vitamins are foods and are normally found in the body. According to Dr. Harold Rosenbert in his great book, *The Doctor's Book on Vitamin Therapy*, there has never been a fatality due to too much of *any* vitamin.

I've done TV shows with some doctors who try to scare people into thinking that anything over 5,000 units of Vitamin A can be harmful, but they've all been amazed when I've pointed out that a 7-ounce portion of beef liver contains 106,800 units of Vitamin A, according to the *United States Department of Agriculture Handbook No. 8, Composition of Foods,* put out by the Agricultural Research Service of the United States; and a 3½-ounce portion of spinach or other cooked greens contains 12,000 units of Vitamin A, so obviously 5,000 units is not too much. Liver is the most nutritious meat you can eat, and many people eat it several times a week and I know some people who eat it every day for lunch or dinner. I take 50,000 units of Vitamin A every day and have for many years and I'm the healthiest person I know.

Vitamin A is essential to good skin—it prevents and clears up skin infections, makes hair shiny, improves day vision and particularly night vision, promotes cell growth, and aids in resisting infections.

Vitamin A and Vitamin E work together, because without Vitamin E, Vitamin A is destroyed by oxygen. Vitamin A is found in green and yellow vegetables and apricots. The National Research Council recommends 5,000 units a day, but as I said, I take 50,000 units a day, and believe that 25,000 units a day should be a bare minimum for an adult.

The B vitamins are B1, B2, B6, B12, biotin, folic acid, inositol, niacin, pantothenic acid, and PABA (para amino benzoic acid). Science is finding there are other B vites, and has recently isolated two, B16 (pangamic acid) and B17 (amygdalin). All the B vites are water-soluble and can't be stored in the body, so they must be taken every day. They are synergistic, which means that one alone or several together increase the need for the rest of them (for instance, if you took lots of B1 or B6, it could make you terribly deficient in all the other B's). When you take the Dynamite Milkshake, you'll be getting *all* the B vites and lots of them because the yeast and lecithin are loaded with them.

Powdered nutritional yeast (brewer's or torula) is all protein and no fat (don't take uncooked baker's yeast by mistake). Powdered yeast has more B vitamins and more all-around nourishment than any other food. I learned about yeast from Adelle Davis' great book, *Let's Eat Right to Keep Fit*, which is the first book on nutrition I ever read. Then I read Linda Clark's terrific book, *Stay Young Longer*, and learned all about lecithin, which has been found to:

1. Reduce cholesterol and help dissolve plaques already in the arteries.
2. Lower blood pressure in some people.
3. Produce more alertness in older people.
4. Increase the gamma globulin in the blood, which fights infection.
5. Help acne, eczema, and psoriasis.
6. Soften aging skin and keep the skin in good shape while reducing.
7. Act as a tranquilizer and help nervous exhaustion.
8. Act as a brain food and help rebuild brain cells (and one study showed that the brain of an insane person had only half as much lecithin in it as a normal brain).
9. Be a sexual aid and restore sexual powers (seminal fluid contains much lecithin).

10. Aid glandular exhaustion and nervous and mental disorders.
11. Redistribute weight, shifting it from unwanted parts to parts where it's needed.
12. Help in the assimilation of Vitamins A and E.
13. Prevent and cure fatty liver.
14. Lengthen the lives of animals and produce healthier coats and more alertness.
15. Lower the requirement of insulin in diabetics (with the additional help of Vitamin E).

Yeast and lecithin are probably the two greatest foods for beautifying the skin, so if you start the milkshake your skin should be gorgeous! Besides making great skin, the B vites are necessary for strong hair, steady nerves and healthy eyes.

Vitamin C is ascorbic acid and Nobel Prize-winner Linus Pauling recommends at least 3,000 mgs a day, but I take a minimum of 10,000 mgs a day and have for years. If I start to sneeze or feel a cold coming on, I go up to 50,000 mgs a day, and several times have taken as much as 100,000 mgs in a day, but I knocked the virus out that same day, and can honestly say that since I've been on high doses of Vitamin C, I haven't been sick even one day (and I used to get colds and flu bugs and viruses maybe eight or ten times a year, bedding me each time for a couple of days—and my doctor bills and antibiotic bills were enormous). Vitamin C is fantastic but you do need massive doses. *If you're taking Vitamin C and still get a cold, then know that you're not taking enough.* And continue taking the large amount of C for at least a day after you start to feel you're all better (and you generally do start to feel better right away after taking a lot of C), because if you stop too soon, the germs will begin to multiply again.

If you have bleeding gums or bruises on your body, these are signs of a Vitamin C deficiency. If you never get a cold or flu bug, then you probably need far less than the rest of us, and 3,000 or 4,000 mgs a day should be enough for you. Vitamin C is water-soluble and can't be stored in the body, so any excess is flushed out, and the body tissues should be saturated with it every day. Be sure to drink lots of liquids when you take lots of Vitamin C. Don't be afraid of taking too much vitamin C—you can't— but do be afraid of not getting enough. Just use your body as a barometer: if you feel great and don't catch colds or viruses, then 3,000 a day is enough— if you do catch colds, etc., then you need more.

A glass of orange juice gives you 100 mgs of Vitamin C, so the only way to get enough is with ascorbic acid tablets, which are less expensive than the "natural" Vitamin C tablets and, according to Linus Pauling, there is no difference chemically. When a virus, flu bug or foreign substance invades the body, it attacks the Vitamin C, destroys it, and is destroyed by it in the process (that's the reason for massive daily doses). Smoking (a foreign substance) uses up 25 mg of Vitamin C per cigarette, so if you smoke, or use aspirin (or any drug remedy), or have any allergy, take plenty of Vitamin C to detoxify them all. It works best when calcium is present in the body, so make sure you drink lots of milk or take calcium/magnesium (dolomite) tablets every day.

Irwin Stone, the biochemist who turned Linus

Pauling on to Vitamin C, wrote a wonderful book, *The Healing Factor: Vitamin C Against Disease.* In it he says that Vitamin C isn't really a vitamin at all, and that every animal on earth—lions, tigers, dogs, cats, lizards—manufacture ascorbic acid in their liver; every animal, that is, except man and the monkey family (and the other primates), a fruit-eating bat in India, and the guinea pig. Through some mutation millions of years ago we lost this ability, and we will die within weeks if we don't add some ascorbic acid to our diet. Irwin Stone recommends that a baby of one year receive 1 gram (1,000 mg) of Vitamin C daily, a child of four 4 grams, a child of ten 10 grams —and then you should stay on 10 grams a day for the rest of your life. Linus Pauling dedicated his great book *Vitamin C and the Common Cold* to Irwin Stone, and I recommend that everyone who wants to learn about his or her body read both Pauling's and Stone's books.

Science has found that many signs thought to be standard for old age are really disease symptoms. Little kids of eight or ten with scurvy (Vitamin C deficiency) lose their teeth and have humped-over shoulders and wrinkly, saggy skin. If you look at pictures of scurvied children, they honestly look like old, old midgets—it's incredible. One of the first signs of scurvy is bleeding gums, and bruises on the body are another sign. So if you bruise easily or your gums ever bleed, increase your Vitamin C till both symptoms disappear.

To me one of the saddest and most ridiculous things about the MDR's (minimum daily requirements) put out by Washington and used by countless doctors all over the country is the MDR on Vitamin C, which is 60 mgs. According to the statistics, 60 mgs of Vitamin C will keep you from getting scurvy, which disease marks the last stage of a Vitamin C deficiency before you *die!* That's like saying the MDR of water is two ounces a day, that that will keep you from dying from a lack of water (or dehydration). Now obviously one wants to be healthier than a borderline case of scurvy, which is one step from death, and the sad part is that so many people accept the MDR's as gospel and are starving their poor bodies from a lack of vitamins, and so many ignorant doctors promote the MDR's as the last word on nutrition. There are lots of great doctors in the world and there are lots of close-minded ones, and if you're wise you'll search out the ones who are open-minded, who are constantly learning about new findings, and who are into preventive medicine and nutrition.

Vitamin D is known as the sunshine vitamin and helps the body absorb calcium and retain it. Without vitamin D, much calcium is lost. Foods don't contain much, so many people are terribly deficient and don't know why they are so nervous. Vitamin D cannot be absorbed without fat or oil, so take it after a meal that includes some oil. Vitamin D, like Vitamin A, can be toxic, but only in massive doses. I take one 50,000-unit capsule of Vitamin D a week. Because you can't buy this amount in a regular store, I have to get it through a pharmicist friend of mine. Dr. J.A. Johnston of the Henry Ford Hospital in Detroit researched Vitamin D, and his studies show that an adult can profit by taking at least 4,000 units daily, so I take over 7,000 units a day (50,000 a week), and this amount is not toxic.

Vitamin E is an oxygenizer and it helps all the muscles in the body by lowering the needs for oxygen. With more oxygen, the heart doesn't have to work as hard. Vitamin E is known as the sex vitamin and helps produce normal sex hormones. Vitamin E also adds oxygen to the brain and has been used to help mentally retarded children. Dr. Del Giudice, head of child psychology at the National Institute of Public Health in Buenos Aires, Argentina, has given mentally retarded children 2,000 to 3,000 units of Vitamin E daily for many years with surprisingly successful results and no evidence of toxicity. If you have high blood pressure, I suggest you start very slowly with 100 units of Vitamin E, and after you've been on the milkshake and vites and have gotten healthier and your blood pressure has lowered, then up your Vitamin E to 400 units. Most everyone else should begin with 800 units, or if you want to start slowly, 400 units and build up to 800. I take 3,600 units a day now (1,200 after each meal) and feel great.

Just remember that vitamins are foods, not drugs (it always amazes me how some doctors warn people about taking vitamins, which are foods and promote great health, and they don't warn people about drinking coffee or eating sugar, both of which are addictive). Once you start to become aware of your body and start to listen to what it's telling you, you'll become sensitive to what it needs, and what to put in and what to keep out. And once you do get to know yourself physically, and your body starts to feel fantastic, you'll begin to really know yourself mentally and emotionally too, and that's the very basis of happiness, because when you really know your self, you can get rid of the negative things and cultivate the positive things and that's when you'll really start to like your self, and life will start to be fun and exciting.

The milkshake and vites aren't a diet—they're truly a way of life. They become as much a habit as shaving or brushing your teeth every day. Everything you put in your body is a cause and will have an effect—some right away, like pimples, headaches, canker sores—and some are long-range effects like strokes, ulcers, heart attacks. When you abuse your gorgeous body, you really can't blame it when it starts to fall apart. But the wonderful thing is that *it's never too late to change.* Even if you've been doing the wrong things for years, you can now begin a new way of life, one that will make you healthier and happier, and when that happens, you'll start to get all the good things in life that you deserve.

Appendix II:

Testimony of Naura Hayden Before the U.S. Congressional Committee on Nutrition, September 27, 1977

To begin with, I'm delighted to be here and I'm honored that Congressman Fred Richmond and his Committee invited me to be part of this hearing. This Committee by its very existence is a progressive body and should be recognized and publicized as a most important part of the Congress, and sitting alongside of you people as the most critical observer should be the President of the United States to hear this important series of testimony.

I'd like to start out and say that there is a Human Energy Crisis and I am disappointed that the present administration hasn't recognized that the lack of human energy is far more of a problem than the shrinking resources of oil.

There are millions of people paid to work eight hours a day who, though willing and ready, are not able to perform more than four or five hours with their coffee breaks, cigarette breaks, candy-bar breaks, sick leave and accidents costing this country billions of dollars.

What a tragedy it would be if we solved the problem of the spiraling economy, cut down crime rates, found jobs for those victims of the recession and then discovered we were plagued with a pooped-out generation of weak, enervated people.

Now I'd like to ask everyone in this room if you feel really super-good and full of energy to raise your hands . . . .

Now, how many of you drink some coffee or cola drink every day? How many of you smoke some cigarettes every day? How many of you eat some sugar every day? How many of you drink a couple of scotches or martinis at lunch or dinner?

I used to need all those things—caffein, nicotine and sugar to rev up my body, and then alcohol to ease the tensions at the end of the day. Those were my "uppers" and "downers" until at a very young age my body gave out and I was hospitalized with not enough energy to walk across a room and that's why I took the time off my acting and singing career to write my book about energy, because I know firsthand what it's like to have a life full of sickness, tension, anxiety and awful depression. I found out firsthand how terrible caffeine is to the body and I wonder why we legalize this drug (and caffeine *is* a drug even though we don't like to admit it, and if you don't believe it, try to cut out all coffee or cola drinks from your life and feel what withdrawal is).

I found out firsthand how addictive sugar is—the more you eat, the more you crave; and again, if you find this hard to believe, try cutting out *all* sugar from your life and you'll see how difficult it is because you *are hooked.*

I would like to take a strong position about sugar. This commercial product, which is taken massively each day, is one of the great sources of illness in this country. It is poisonous to the system. We find it difficult to believe that something mummy and daddy gave us can be so harmful, but mummy and daddy have been misled by the sugar industry just like all the rest of us.

It seems ironic that very little is ever done to publicize and pinpoint the bad effects of sugar, while there has been a concerted effort to discredit sugar substitutes. There certainly seems to be a motivation behind this method of perpetuating sugar at any cost. The tests against saccharin have been inconclusive and yet wholesale scare tactics were inserted to make people think a few sips of a non-sugared soft drink will cause cancer. If the rats in the saccharin studies had been fed the equivalent amount of sugar I believe it would have killed them and I believe it is imperative that sugar be tested using the same enormous amounts that were used with saccharin.

Of course, we all know alcohol is a drug and there are millions of social drinkers and millions more who are "closet" drinkers and alcoholics, ashamed to let the world know their bodies are addicted to this drug.

Why is it so many Americans are hooked on caffeine, nicotine, sugar and alcohol? It's because their bodies are malnourished and have no energy, so they put in the junk which gives a short lift and then unfortunately plummets them down. This is like whipping a tired horse and proves we are an overfed and undernourished nation.

I have been fortunate to travel to over thirty-three cities many times in the past twelve months on tour with my "Energy" book, and I have met and talked with thousands of people on TV shows, radio shows and in stores and I found out that the majority of people don't feel good. They are tense, depressed and sick a lot of the time and they are tired of being tired. But more than that, they are confused because when they go to their doctors and ask why they're tense, the doctors are too quick to give tranquilizers and when they're tired and depressed the doctors are too quick to give "uppers," and like all drugs, the more you take the worse you feel. Now, of course, not all doctors are "drug-happy." There are some fine doctors who are into preventive medicine, but most doctors are trained in medical school to treat you with drugs once you are already sick—but what about teaching these doctors how to *prevent* disease and how to build strong, healthy, energetic bodies through nutrition and vitamins?

How many times a day in how many doctors' offices are there prescriptions given for drugs instead of vitamins and food supplements that if taken regularly can prevent sickness? There is something drastically wrong when so many doctors through ignorance scare people about eggs and milk and vitamins which are good foods and build health, and not about coffee, sugar and alcohol.

There is also a lot of confusion in children's minds. They are inundated with TV ads telling them that sugar-coated cereals are good for them and they'll get all the vitamins and nutrition from these kinds of junk foods, but these ads aren't just misleading, they're downright lies.

We need courses in *every* school in America to teach all kids about what vitamins are and why we need them and which foods build strong healthy bodies to play soccer and little league and fuel their brains so they can think more clearly—and which foods are junk and how they cause bad grades, mental disorders, weakened muscles and disease.

If I seem passionate about nutrition and vitamins, it's because I am. Only someone who has suffered with illness can really appreciate great health and I want to turn everybody on to what I have learned so that *everybody* can feel as good as *I* do.

If some of you think I'm exaggerating, you are wrong. If you went around the country and got the enormous response I've gotten you'd realize how desperate people are for information about how to heal their sick bodies and depressed minds. They're tired of giving money to doctors and psychiatrists and feeling worse.

I believe the time is now to face up to the truth. Caffeine, nicotine, sugar and alcohol are injurious to the body and we have got to stand up and say so. I had to heal myself of all the illnesses plaguing me, but before I did I spent thousands of dollars on doctor bills and drugs. I suffered needlessly with depression until I found out about nutrition and vitamins and totally cured myself. I am now the healthiest person I know, *and* the most energetic. I have received over 15,000 letters so far in the last year from people all over the country relating how they're changing their lives through nutrition and vitamins and are feeling good for the first time ... In summation, thanking the Committee for an opportunity to be heard, I would like to stress the need for *intense nutritional training* made *mandatory* at every medical school in the country, the need for mandatory nutritional training in every *grammar* and *high* school in the country, an in-depth study on the effects of sugar given the same intense publicity as the studies on saccharin. I would like to see a special tax placed on foods which do *not* contain the nutrients necessary to sustain health, and the same warning put on these non-nutritious foods that is put on cigarettes—a warning that they are dangerous to your health.

I do hope there are some persuasive congressmen and women and senators who can convince President Jimmy Carter that the Human Energy Crisis is more important than the Panama Canal, the economy or any other national problem. I think it should be a top priority in his next six months in office.

If volunteers are needed to participate in this program, let me go on record and state that for less than the expected dollar a year, I enlist.

Thank you.

NAURA HAYDEN

Bibliography

IN MY *"energy"* book I suggested some terrific books for you to read—books that helped to change my life for the better. Here are some more books that I think you'll find fantastic to read.

1. *Emotional Common Sense* by Rolland Parker, Ph.D.
   Common sense is a terrific start for dealing with your feelings.
2. *Learning to Love Again* by Mel Krantzler
   A good book for all of us looking for a loving commitment.
3. *Self Creation* by Dr. George Weinberg
   Who better to start creating into a stronger, better, more confident person than your self?
4. *On Caring* by Milton Mayeroff
   This book shows that we aren't at home in the world through dominating, or explaining, or appreciating, but through caring and being cared for.

5. *The Doctor's Book of Vitamin Therapy* by Dr. Harold Rosenberg and A. N. Feldzamen, Ph.D.
   This is one of the best books on vites and minerals I've ever read.

6. *Love* by Leo Buscaglia
   A beautiful book truly full of love and the things learned in a "Love Class."

7. *Mega-Nutrients* by H. L. Newbold, M.D.
   Written by a psychiatrist, this book is especially about your nervous system, and goes into detail about allergies and total nutrition.

8. *You* by Frances Wilshire
   This is one of my all-time favorite books that I've been reading for years, and it tells all about how to get to know yourself.

9. *The Human Miracle* by Loriene Chase, Ph.D. and Clifton W. King
   An unusual self-help book that tells about meditation, dream analysis and dream-to-order techniques.

10. *Super Nutrition for Healthy Hearts* by Richard Passwater, Ph.D.
    Written by a biochemist, it's not only great for your heart, but also for every other part of your body.

11. *Restoring the American Dream* by Robert Ringer
    A fantastic book about what this great country is really all about and what we can do to keep it great.

12. *Food Facts and Fallacies* by Carlton Fredericks, Ph.D. and Herbert Bailey
    A good book to help us all achieve a better

physical and mental life through proper nutrition.

13. *Of Love and Lust* by Theodor Reik
    If you want to explore the mysteries of love and sex by this world-renowned psychoanalyst, you'll read this.

14. *The Secret of Staying in Love* by John Powell, S.J.
    A wonderful book about love and communication and human needs and the sharing of feelings.

15. *Self Analysis* by Karen Horney
    This is one of the best books about psychoanalysis and how to analyze yourself, written by one of the most well-known psychiatrists in the world.

16. *Love and Hate in Human Nature* by Arnold A. Hutschnecker, M.D.
    Dr. Hutschnecker shows how to understand emotional upsets and possibly avoid illness.

17. *How to Survive the Loss of a Love* by Melba Colgrove, Ph.D., Harold H. Bloomfield, M.D., and Peter McWilliams.
    This book will help you survive:
    1) death of a loved one
    2) loss of a job
    3) breakup of an affair
    4) loss of money
    5) divorce
    6) loss of hair
    and any other awful loss.

18. *Nutrigenetics* by Dr. R. O. Brennan with William C. Mulligan

This book will help you feel better and live longer.

19. *Your Fear of Love* by Marshall Bryant Hodge
This is a book about how to be free and how to accept ourselves.

Isle of View is a place in your heart and when you go there you feel loving and lovable and loved.

These feelings of love are contagious, so let's start an epidemic.

Isle of View.